PCs

by Shelley O'Hara
and Galen A. Grimes

A Division of Macmillan Computer Publishing
201 W. 103rd Street, Indianapolis, Indiana 46290 USA

PCs Cheat Sheet

© 1999 by Que® Corporation

International Standard Book Number: 0-7897-1874-X

Library of Congress Catalog Card Number: 98-87210

Printed in the United States of America

First Printing: *March 1999*

01 00   4

Interpretation of the printing code: the rightmost number of the first series of numbers is the year of the book's printing; the rightmost number of the second series of numbers is the number of the book's printing. For example, a printing code of 98-1 shows that the first printing of the book occured in 1998.

Trademarks

Executive Editor *Angela Wethington*

Acquisitions Editor *Jamie Milazzo*

Development Editor *Joyce Nielsen*

Technical Editor *Kyle Bryant*

Managing Editor *Thomas F. Hayes*

Project Editor *Sossity Smith*

Copy Editor *Shanon Martin*

Indexer *Cheryl Landis*

Proofreaders *Maribeth Echard, Christy M. Lemasters, Nicole Ritch*

Layout Technician *Christy M. Lemasters*

Contents at a Glance

Part 4 Setup and Customization

Part 5 PC Maintenance

Part 6 Connecting to the Internet

Part 7 Networking

Contents

Part 2 Program Basics

Part 3 File Basics

Part 4 Setup and Customization

Part 5 PC Maintenance

Part 7 Networking

About the Authors

Shelley O'Hara is the author of over 70 books, mostly relating to computers. Several of the books, including *Easy Windows 98*, have become bestsellers. O'Hara has a BA in English from the University of South Carolina and an MA in English from the University of Maryland. She lives in Indianapolis with her husband Sean, son Michael, and English Bulldog Jelly Roll.

Galen A. Grimes is the author of several books, including *Sams Teach Yourself Upgrading and Fixing PCs in 24 Hours* and the *Ten Minute Guide to Netscape Communicator 4*. Galen has been working with computers since 1980 when he purchased his first PC, an Apple II+. Since then he has worked on PCs using DOS, Windows (3.1/95/NT 4.0), and UNIX and has programmed in about a dozen different programming languages including C/C++, Assembler, Pascal, BASIC, and xBase. Galen has a masterís degree in Information Science from the University of Pittsburgh and is currently a computer systems project manager at Mellon Bank in Pittsburgh, PA.

Dedication

To my dad and hero, Raymond Neff Ball.—S.O.

Acknowledgments

Thanks to Joyce Nielsen for her insightful comments and helpful suggestions.

Tell Us What You Think!

As the reader of this book, *you* are our most important critic and commentator. We value your opinion and want to know what we're doing right, what we could do better, what areas you'd like to see us publish in, and any other words of wisdom you're willing to pass our way.

As the Executive Editor for the Desktop Applications team at Macmillan Computer Publishing, I welcome your comments. You can fax, email, or write me directly to let me know what you did or didn't like about this book—as well as what we can do to make our books stronger.

Please note that I cannot help you with technical problems related to the topic of this book, and that due to the high volume of mail I receive, I might not be able to reply to every message.

When you write, please be sure to include this book's title and author as well as your name and phone or fax number. I will carefully review your comments and share them with the author and editors who worked on the book.

Fax: 317-817-7448

Email: pcs@mcp.com

Mail: Executive Editor
        General Desktop Applications
        Macmillan Computer Publishing
        201 West 103rd Street
        Indianapolis, IN 46290 USA

Introduction

Using a computer is supposed to make things easier, but you may not have time to wade through a big, fat manual to find the information you need. You need to know just the basics—just the stuff to get by in your day-to-day work. You need a cheat sheet. And that's this book.

What Makes This Book Different?

This book is designed to make using a computer as easy as possible. The book weeds out extraneous information and focuses on the skills you need to use your PC most effectively. Following are the key benefits of this book:

- The key concepts and commands are highlighted, helping you identify the most important information.

- This book doesn't cover each and every feature. It covers the features you are most likely to use and will get the most benefit from.

- This book is divided into more than 50 short chapters that deal with a particular topic. Finding the information you need is easy.

- Each chapter starts with a Cheat Sheet—a quick list of the most important information and steps in the chapter.

- Within each chapter, the most basic tasks are covered first in a section called "Basic Survival." When you are getting started, concentrate on these sections.

- After the "Basic Survival" section, you find a "Beyond Survival" section that covers the topic in a little more detail. Check out these sections when you want to learn more about a topic.

- For every task, you find step-by-step instructions, illustrated with figures so that you can easily follow along. **Note:** The figures in this book show Windows 98. If you have Windows 95, you might see something slightly different.

- You can find tips in the margins, reminders of important notes, cautions, and shortcuts.

How This Book Is Organized

This book is organized into several parts:

Part 1, "Computer Basics," covers the basic information about using a computer—what a computer is, how to start and shut down the PC, what you see when the PC starts, and more.

Part 2, "Program Basics," explains all you need to know to get started using most programs. You not only learn how to start programs, but also some key skills that work from one program to the next.

Part 3, "File Basics," describes how to manage the files on your computer. You can find information on how to copy, rename, delete, and otherwise handle the files on your system.

Part 4, "Setup and Customization," covers some of the different ways you can change how your PC works. You can find features that make your work easier or more pleasing to you.

Part 5, "PC Maintenance," focuses on some tasks that you might not do every day, but should do every now and then. You find out how to check your hard drive for errors, back up important files, install new hardware, and more.

Part 6, "Connecting to the Internet," takes you beyond your own computer to the wide world of the Internet. You learn what you need to get connected as well as what you can do once connected.

Part 7, "Networking," is written for users that are connected to a network. You can read about networking issues, such as sharing files and printers.

PART

1

Computer Basics

If you aren't sure what pieces and parts make up a computer, how to start or set up a computer, or how to use Windows, read this part. This part explains all the basics of using a PC. The following topics are covered:

- Computers Defined
- Basic Hardware Defined
- Drives Defined
- Software Defined
- Setting Up Your PC
- Turning the PC On and Off
- Understanding the Windows Desktop
- Selecting Commands
- Working with Windows
- Getting Help

Cheat Sheet

Hardware   The physical components of your computer, including the system box, monitor, keyboard, and mouse.

Software   The instructions that enable your computer to perform tasks.

Operating system   The software that enables your computer to work. You use the operating system to run and install programs, to manage files, and more.

Notebook   A smaller version of a PC, about the size of a school notebook (10"×12").

Laptop   A portable version of a PC, similar to a notebook, but bigger.

Computers Defined

A *computer* is an electronic appliance—such as a TV, VCR, or dryer—that you use to do some task. The thrilling thing about a computer is that you can use it to do many types of tasks—write letters, draw a map, play a game, and more.

You don't really have to know a lot about how a computer works to use it. Think about your car. Your car works because of the different elements that make up the car: the engine, the transmission, the wheels, and so on. You don't need to understand exactly how a car works to drive it. A PC is the same. It is actually a group of components working together.

Basically, a PC is the hardware—the physical components that you can see and touch—and the software—the programming instructions that make the physical components work.

Basic Survival

What Is Hardware?

The items that you unpack and actually touch are the *hardware* components. The hardware consists of the system box, monitor, keyboard, mouse, and other physical components. Chapters 2, "Basic Hardware Defined," and 3, "Drives Defined," cover hardware in more detail.

What Is Software?

Software is the program instructions that turn your PC into anything you want it to be. With the applicable software, you can use your PC to write letters, create reports, draw illustrations, make a presentation, balance your checkbook, and more. You can find many different types of software. Chapter 4, "Software Defined," describes some basic types of applications.

Beyond Survival

Types of PCs

Basically, you can purchase two types of computers: an IBM or compatible, and a Macintosh. Around 80 percent of the computers sold are IBMs or compatibles, and the term PC usually refers to this type of computer. At one time, there used to be a difference in quality between an IBM and an IBM-compatible, but now you find the most popular PCs are IBM-compatibles. You can find companies such as Dell, Gateway, Micron, and others that manufacture best-selling PCs.

Most PCs use Windows 95, Windows 98, or Windows NT (mostly a networking version of Windows) as the operating system.

A Macintosh differs from an IBM or IBM-compatible mainly because of the operating system. This type of computer uses a different operating system, called System. Although you can share data files from a PC to a Macintosh, you cannot run software programs created for Windows on a Macintosh or vice versa. The Macintosh also uses a different microprocessor. (For information on microprocessors, see the next chapter.)

This book covers IBMs and compatibles because they are the primary PC market.

Laptop and Notebook Computers

If you use your PC in one spot such as your home or office, you most likely have a desktop or tower model. If, on the other hand, you travel and want to take your PC with you, you may decide to purchase a portable PC.

With a portable PC, all the elements are compacted and combined into one unit so that it is easy to carry. The difference between portable models is the size.

A *notebook* computer is about the size of a school notebook (10"×12") and can weigh as little as four to six pounds. You could fit a notebook PC in your briefcase. A *laptop* computer is similar to a notebook computer, but is bigger. It's usually thicker and weighs more.

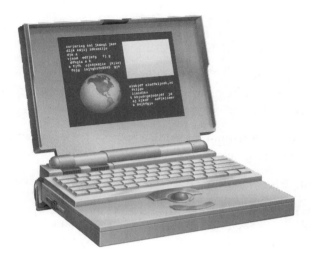

If you are thinking that smaller is less expensive, think again. Because a lot of complex technology is required to cram all the components into a small package, most notebooks and laptops are more expensive than a comparable desktop system. If you need a notebook PC, then certainly get one. But if you don't really need one, you get more power and performance from a similarly priced desktop model.

Cheat Sheet

Key Terms

Microprocessor   The most important part of the computer. Part of the motherboard (the main electronic board inside the system unit). Determines the speed and features of a PC.

Memory   A temporary holding spot for your data and programs. Your computer has memory chips inside, housed on the motherboard.

Disk drives   A permanent storage place for your data and programs.

Expansion slots   Slots inside the PC into which you can insert electronic cards (sometimes called expansion cards) to add features such as an internal modem or sound card.

Monitor   The TV-like thing you look at. The monitor is actually two parts: the display and the electronic card (video adapter) inside the system unit.

Dot-matrix printer   A printer type that works by firing pins against a ribbon to make dots on the page.

Inkjet printer   Works by spraying tiny dots of ink on a page through a tiny nozzle.

Laser printer   Uses a toner cartridge and works similar to a copy machine.

Using the Mouse

- **Point**   Move the mouse on the desk until the pointer is in the spot you want.
- **Click**   Press the left mouse button once.
- **Right-click**   Point to the item and press the right mouse button.
- **Double-click**   Point to the item and press the left mouse button twice in rapid succession.
- **Drag**   Click and hold down the left mouse button and then drag the mouse.

2

Basic Hardware Defined

When you purchase a PC, the following components are included: system unit, monitor, keyboard, and mouse. You may also have a printer.

Basic Survival

The System Box

Probably the biggest element of your computer is the *system box*. The system box houses all the electronic wizardry that make up a PC. Here's what you would find if you opened up the box and took a look inside:

- **Microprocessor** The most important part of the computer is the microprocessor. You can think of this chip as the computer's "brain." The microprocessor is part of the motherboard (the main electronic board inside the system unit) and determines the speed and features of a PC. Most everything hooks up to the motherboard.

- **Memory** When you run a program or create a document, the information is stored in memory, a temporary holding spot. Your computer has memory chips inside, housed on the motherboard.

- **Disk drives** You need a more permanent storage place for your data and programs, and this place is your hard drive. In addition to a hard drive, your system probably has a floppy drive and possibly a CD-ROM drive. (You learn all about drives in Chapter 3, "Drives Defined.")

- **Power supply** To power all the elements inside the system box, you need a power supply. This box is housed inside the system unit, too.

- **Expansion slots** So that you can add features to your PC, your system has expansion slots. You can insert electronic cards (sometimes called expansion cards) into these slots. Some slots may already be taken with such features as an internal modem or a sound card.

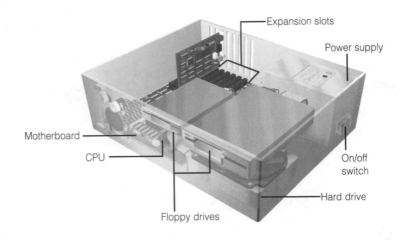

The Monitor

The *monitor* is the TV-like box that displays what you are working on. The monitor shows programs onscreen. What you type also appears in the program window on the monitor. To use the monitor, flip the power switch. You may also make some adjustments to the display using the control knobs on the front of the monitor.

A monitor is actually two hardware components working together. You have the box that sits on your desk, and you have a video card inside the PC. The video card and motherboard are connected via a controller. The video card and the monitor are connected via a plug on the back of the PC.

Monitors differ in a few key ways: size, quality of the image (or resolution), and the standard. The easiest thing to understand is the size. Monitors are measured diagonally like TVs. Most new monitors are usually 13 inches or bigger. (The bigger the monitor, the more you can see onscreen.)

Resolution, the quality of the displayed image, is a little trickier. Computer monitors measure the number of pixels or dots per inch that a monitor can display horizontally and vertically. You may see this as 640×480, 800×600, or 1,024×768. With some monitors, you can select which resolution is used. The higher the number, the more dots per inch and the sharper the image.

Another monitor term you may hear is the *standard.* Most monitors today are VGA or SuperVGA (SVGA). The standard controls the number of colors and resolution a particular monitor can display.

The Keyboard

To enter information—type text, select commands, and so on—you use the keyboard. Most keyboards look about the same and have about the same number of keys. The most popular keyboard is the 101-key keyboard.

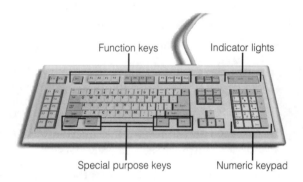

Function keys   Indicator lights

Special purpose keys   Numeric keypad

You use the keyboard like a typewriter: Simply press the keys. In addition to alphanumeric characters, the keyboard also includes special keys you can use for shortcuts in programs. Different keys do different things, depending on the program. For instance, pressing the F1 key in most programs displays the Help contents.

A keyboard also has a numeric keypad, which you can use to enter numbers (press the Num Lock key) or move the cursor.

To avoid repetitive stress injuries sometimes associated with typing (such as carpal tunnel syndrome), you can buy a special type of keyboard designed to support your wrists while you type. Microsoft, for instance, sells this type of ergonomical keyboard.

The Mouse

Before Windows became the standard operating system, most commands were typed. Therefore, all you needed was a keyboard. Windows, because it is a graphical user interface, required an additional way to make choices. Windows enabled you to point to what you wanted. The input device for pointing and selecting is the mouse.

Now, the mouse is standard equipment on a PC. You can use the mouse to select menu commands, start programs, open windows, manipulate windows, and more.

Many beginners have trouble getting the hang of the mouse, but once you get some practice, you find that it comes natural. Following are the basic mouse moves:

- **Point** Move the mouse on the desk until the pointer is in the spot you want.

- **Click** To click, press the left mouse button once. Most mice have more than one button. The left button is used most often. You may find some shortcuts that you can access by using the right mouse button. Point to the item and click the right mouse button. (If you are left-handed, you can reverse the functions of the left and right mouse buttons. See Chapter 35.)

- **Double-click** Press the mouse button twice in rapid succession.

- **Drag** Click and hold down the mouse button and then drag the mouse. You use this dragging motion to select text, move items, and perform other tasks.

A good way to practice using the mouse is to play Solitaire.

Many different companies manufacture mouse devices, including Microsoft. The newest Microsoft mouse is called the IntelliMouse and includes additional features that software programs can take advantage of. For instance, many of the Microsoft Office programs use the IntelliMouse for scrolling shortcuts.

The Printer

When you purchase a new PC, you can expect that PC to include the system unit and all its contents: the monitor, the keyboard, and the mouse. This is a typical PC setup. In addition to these elements, you may also purchase a printer. You most likely use your PC to create some type of document, and more often than not, you want to print that document.

The following list describes each of the main types of printers:

- A laser printer offers the fastest printing and better quality than any other printing. On the downside, it is usually a bit more expensive than other printer types. The price range and feature list of laser printers can vary greatly. You can find a simple, reasonably priced desktop model or a big, fast, network printer.

- You can think of inkjet printers as the middle of the road. Inkjet printers don't offer the same quality as a laser printer, but they are better than dot-matrix printers. They are usually in between the two in cost also. An inkjet printer works by spraying tiny dots on a page through a tiny nozzle. The quality of the printout is usually pretty good, and the price is often reasonable. If you want a color printer, inkjet color printers are especially worth considering.

- Dot-matrix printers used to be the most popular type of printer because they were the least expensive. As prices have dropped for other printer types, the popularity of this type of printer has declined. You may still find this printer, though, used for printing multipart forms. A dot-matrix printer works by firing pins against a ribbon to make dots on the page. The combination of dots form characters and graphics. In terms of quality, dot-matrix printers are at the bottom of the totem pole.

Beyond Survival

System Box Types

When discussing types of PCs, you may hear the term *tower model* or *desktop model*. This description refers to the style of the system box. A tower model sits upright on your floor. A desktop model sits horizontally on your desk. The orientation of the system box is the only thing that is different. The components and how they work are the same.

More on the Microprocessor

The most important part of a computer is the microprocessor chip, sometimes called the CPU (central processing unit) or simply processor. This tiny chip, the size of a cracker, determines the power of a computer. The two most important distinctions of the microprocessor are the name, or type, of chip and the speed.

Originally, processor chips were named with numbers—the higher the number, the more powerful the chip. Following is a breakdown of the history of the microprocessor, from the earliest processor used in PCs to the newest:

8088	Used in the original IBM PC. Now obsolete.
8086	Used in the older Compaqs and other PCs. Now obsolete.
80286	Used in the AT computers. Now obsolete.
80386	Introduced and gained popularity in the late '80s. Now obsolete.
80486	Introduced in 1991. Now obsolete.
Pentium	Basically, an 80586 chip. Sometimes called the P5. Now obsolete.
Pentium MMX	A Pentium chip with enhanced multimedia capabilities.
Pentium Pro	Basically, an 80686 chip or P6.
Pentium II	The newest generation of Pentium. A Pentium Pro chip with MMX capabilities.

If you recently purchased a PC, you probably have a Pentium II. If you have an older PC or a used PC, you may have a PC that uses an older chip. How can you tell? Look at the system box. Usually, you can find the processor type and speed (covered next) somewhere on the box.

The speed of the chip is rated in *megahertz* (MHz). One megahertz equals one million clock ticks per second. The higher the megahertz, the faster the computer. Most chips are available in different speeds, and you pay more for the faster computer.

More on Memory

After the microprocessor, the next most important component of the computer is the amount of memory, or *RAM*, it has. RAM stands for random access memory and is the working area of the computer where the computer stores instructions and data. The bigger the working area (that is, more memory), the better.

RAM is measured in bytes. One *kilobyte* (abbreviated K or KB) equals roughly 1,000 bytes. (One kilobyte actually equals 1,024 bytes, but the numbers are rounded.) One *megabyte* (abbreviated M or MB) equals 1,000,000 bytes. One *gigabyte* (abbreviated G or GB) equals one billion bytes. If you bought a new PC today, you could expect to find PCs with anywhere from 32M to 128M or more of RAM.

It's easy to forget just how much memory your system has. If you aren't sure, you can display the amount of memory (as well as the processor type) by following these steps:

1. On the Windows desktop, right-click the My Computer icon.

2. From the shortcut menu that appears, select Properties.

   You see the System Properties dialog box, which displays some information about your system, including the amount of memory.

Windows version

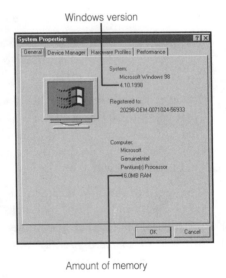

Amount of memory

3. Click the Cancel button to close the dialog box.

Cheat Sheet

Key Terms

Floppy drive   The drive you use to get data and programs onto your hard drive. You can also copy data files from your hard disk to a floppy disk so that you can take the floppy disk with you.

Hard drive   The drive housed inside your system unit and used for storing programs and data files.

CD-ROM drive   Another type of drive used for running programs and copying data from the CD to your hard drive.

DVD-ROM drive   Another new type of drive used for distributing programs (and movies).

Viewing the Drives on Your System

1. Double-click the My Computer icon on the desktop.
2. Review the information and then click the Close (X) button to close the window.

Finding Out the Size of a Drive

1. Double-click the My Computer icon on the desktop.
2. Right-click the icon for your hard drive.
3. From the submenu that appears, select Properties.
4. Review the information and then click OK.

Formatting a Floppy Disk

1. Insert the disk you want to format into the drive.
2. Double-click the My Computer icon on the Windows desktop.
3. Right-click your floppy drive (usually Drive A) and select Format.
4. If necessary, display the Capacity drop-down list and select the correct capacity for your disk.
5. Select the type of format.
6. If you want, enter a label into the Label text box.
7. Click the Start button.
8. When you see a message telling you the format is complete, click OK.

Drives Defined

Computers need a place to store information (files and programs) and that place is on a disk drive. When you save a file, the information is recorded magnetically onto the drive's surface. When you want to use that information again, the disk reads the information from the drive. On most new PCs, you can expect to have a floppy drive, hard drive, and CD-ROM drive.

Basic Survival

Floppy Drives

Your hard disk is the primary storage space for programs or files. Therefore, you need a way to get programs onto the hard disk. And what if you want to take a file with you—say take a file from your office PC to your home PC? A floppy disk drive provides the medium for moving information onto and off of your hard drive.

Older PCs used a different type of floppy drive. The disks were 5 1/4" in size and were actually floppy. As technology advanced, a new type of floppy disk became popular. This type of disk is 3 1/2" in size and is encased in hard plastic.

Disks vary in the amount of information they can store (called the capacity). The capacity is measured in megabytes (MB) or kilobytes (KB). You can find 5 1/4" disks in 360KB and 1.2MB size. The 3 1/2" disks come in two capacities: 720KB and 1.44MB. If you have a 3 1/2" drive, you can use either the 720KB or the 1.44MB disk.

Zip drives use a different type of technology to fit more information (100MB) on a disk.

If you have a fairly new PC, you probably have just one floppy drive, and it is probably a 3 1/2" drive. Drives have names, and if you have one drive, your floppy drive is named A drive. Older PCs may have two floppy drives: A drive and B drive.

As technology advances, newer types of floppy drives are emerging. You can, for instance, purchase a Zip drive. This type of disk and drive can store even more information than the standard 3 1/2" floppy disk and drive.

To insert a disk into the drive, slide it label up into the drive until you hear a click. To eject a disk, press the disk drive button.

Hard Drives

All PCs come with a hard disk, and you store your programs and data files on this hard disk. The hard disk is housed inside the system unit. Most systems have just one hard disk, but you can always add another—either another internal drive housed in the system unit or an external drive that is connected to the PC via a cable.

Like the floppy drive, the hard drive has a name, and it is usually C drive.

Drives differ in a few key ways. The most important distinction is size (again, called the capacity). Hard drives are measured in megabytes (MB) or gigabytes (GB). The bigger the drive, the better. You will be surprised how fast your drive fills up with programs and files!

Drives also differ in how fast they are—that is, how fast the drive takes to find and access information. The speed is measured in milliseconds (ms). Anything in the 8–12ms range is a good speed.

CD-ROM and DVD-ROM Drives

Floppy disks can only store so much information. Therefore, a newer method for distributing information emerged: CD-ROM discs. CD-ROM discs can store much more information than a regular floppy disk; they can store over 700MB of data. But, although you can both read and write information to a floppy disk, you can only read the data from a CD-ROM. (ROM stands for read-only memory.)

CD-ROMs became popular and standard equipment on PCs when multimedia became popular. Multimedia programs combine text, video, graphics, and sound. Because video, graphic, and sound files are really big, CD-ROM discs became ideal for distributing information such as programs, encyclopedias, and other large collections of information.

If you have a newer PC, you most likely have a CD-ROM drive as part of your system. Usually this drive is housed inside the system unit, and like other drives has a name. If you have just one hard drive, your CD-ROM drive is most likely D drive.

CD-ROM drives differ in their speed. You often see the speed advertised as 24×. That's 24 times as fast as the original 1× drive's speed. Speed measurements such as 24× can be arbitrary. If you really want to know the speed, find out the access time and transfer time.

New versions of CD drives are available that enable you to both read and write data to a CD disc.

To insert a disc into the drive, you press the Eject button and then lay the disc (label side up) inside the drive. Press the drive door to insert the disc. Some drives have a cartridge. Insert the disc into the cartridge and then insert the cartridge into the drive.

Another newer type of drive is also available—DVD-ROM drives. These drives can read CD-ROMs as well as DVD discs, another method for storing and distributing data and programs.

Beyond Survival

What Drives Do You Have?

Which drives do you have? A quick way to find out is to open My Computer. You should see drive icons for each of the drives on your system. Follow these steps:

1. Double-click the My Computer icon on the desktop. You see the contents of your system, including icons for each drive. You also see some system folders.

2. Click the Close (X) button to close the window.

What Size Hard Drive?

When you first purchased your PC, you probably knew the size of the drive, but after you've had your PC awhile, you may not remember the size. You also may want to review how much space is taken and how much space is free. You can quickly review this and other hard drive information using Windows. Follow these steps:

1. Double-click the My Computer icon on the desktop.

2. Right-click the icon for your hard drive.

3. From the submenu that appears, select Properties. You see the Properties dialog box. You can see the capacity of the drive, the space used, and the space free.

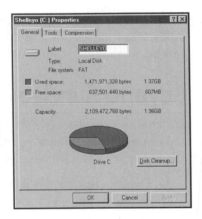

4. Review the information and then click the OK button.

Formatting a Floppy Disk

Before you can use a floppy disk, you must prepare it for use, and this process is called *formatting*. Formatting divides the disk up into storage units, where the data will be saved. You can purchase preformatted floppy disks to save time. If you did not purchase preformatted disks or you want to format an existing disk, you can do so using Windows. Follow these steps:

Formatting erases all the information on a disk.

1. Insert the disk you want to format into the drive.

2. Double-click the My Computer icon on the Windows desktop.

3. Right-click your floppy drive (usually A drive) and select the Format command. You see the Format dialog box.

Select the
format type.

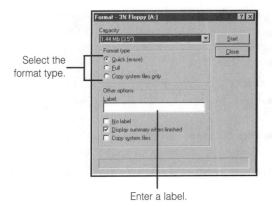

Enter a label.

4. If necessary, display the Capacity drop-down list and select the correct capacity for your disk.

5. Select the type of format. The Quick option formats the disk and erases all the files. This method does not check the disk for bad sectors. The Full option erases the files, prepares the disk, and checks for bad sectors. The Copy System Files Only option adds the system files to the disk so that you can use this disk to start your PC.

6. If you want, enter a label into the Label text box. This label appears when the disk is displayed in a window.

7. Click the Start button.

8. When you see a message telling you the format is complete, click the OK button.

After the floppy is formatted, you can use it to store files.

Cheat Sheet

Basic Types of Programs

- **Word processing**   Use to create documents such as letters, memos, reports, manuscripts, and so on. If there was something you would have formerly done on a typewriter, you now use a word processing program for the task.
- **Spreadsheets**   Enables you to enter and manipulate all kinds of financial information: budgets, sales statistics, income, expenses, and so on.
- **Database programs**   Use to track and manage any set of data: clients, inventory, orders, events, and so on.
- **Presentation programs**   Use to create slides, handouts, and notes for a presentation.
- **Internet programs**   Use to hook up to and view content on the Internet.
- **Personal Information Managers (PIMs)**   Use to keep track of people, events, appointments, places, and so on.
- **Games and educational software**   Two other broad categories that enable you to use your PC for fun and learning.
- **Desktop publishing programs**   Enable you greater control over the layout of a page.
- **Drawing programs**   Use to create and manipulate graphic images.
- **Utility programs**   Use to fine-tune your computer.

4

Software Defined

The *software* is the magic that makes the computer such a useful tool. With the right application, you can use your computer for so many different types of tasks. To use any type of application, you must have basic system software, called the *operating system*.

Basic Survival

What Is an Operating System?

To handle the communication between the different hardware components, you need a system program, called the operating system. The operating system handles such things as starting programs, storing files, printing documents, and so on.

All computers come with an operating system, and the most popular operating system is Windows. The current version of Windows is Windows 98, but you may have a previous version such as Windows 95. If you are using a network version of Windows, you may have Windows NT.

When you start your computer, you see the operating system. From here, you can then start the program you want to use.

Find out more about Windows later in this part.

Most of your time spent using your computer won't be spent actually in Windows; although Windows is busy in the background handling all the behind-the-scenes type of work. Most of your time spent using a PC is spent using some type of application.

Popular Application Programs

To perform a certain type of task using your computer—for instance, typing a letter—you need an application or program for that task. When you purchase a new PC, you may receive some applications as part of the purchase. Windows also includes some mini-applications. These applications get you started. You may also want to purchase additional applications as you learn to do more with your PC.

The terms program, application, or any combination (such as application program) are used interchangeably. They all mean the same thing.

The following list describes the most common types of programs:

- **Word processing** The most common type of application is word processing. You can use this type of program to create documents such as letters, memos, reports, manuscripts, and so on. If there was something you would have formerly done on a typewriter, you now use a word processing program for the task. Word processing programs are more than just a fancy typewriter, though. They offer many editing and formatting features so that you have a great deal of control over the content and look of your document.

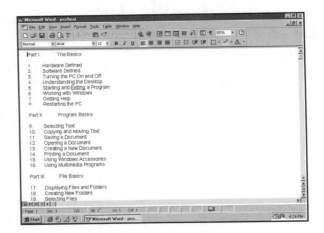

- **Spreadsheets** If numbers are your game, then you will most likely work with a spreadsheet application. This type of program enables you to enter and manipulate all kinds of financial information: budgets, sales statistics, income, expenses, and so on. You enter these figures in a *worksheet*—a grid of columns and rows. The intersection of a row and column is called a *cell*, and you enter text, numbers, or formulas into the cells to create a worksheet.

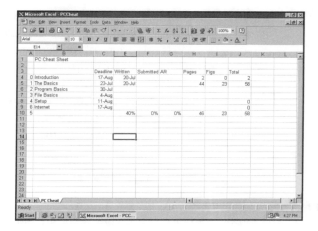

- **Database** You can use a database program to track
  and manage any set of data: clients, inventory, orders,
  events, and so on. Database programs vary from simple
  list managers to complex programs you can use to manage linked systems of information. Databases offer a lot
  of advantages when you are working with large amounts
  of information. First, you can easily search for and find a
  particular piece of information. Second, you can sort the
  data into a different order, as needed. Sort a client list
  alphabetically for a phone list. Sort by zip code for a
  mailing. Third, you can work with subsets of the data:
  all clients in Indiana, all clients that ordered more than
  $10,000 worth of products, and so on.

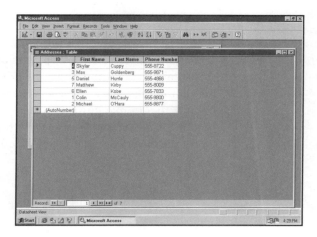

One of the recent trends in software is to create a package or suite of the most popular programs and sell them together. For example, Microsoft offers several versions of Office, its suite of applications. The standard Microsoft Office suite includes Word, Excel, PowerPoint, and Outlook. The professional edition also includes Access. Corel and Lotus offer similar suites that include their most popular word processing, spreadsheet, database, and presentation programs.

Beyond Survival

Other Types of Programs

When most people get started, they use one or two of the basic program types. But if your needs are more specialized, if you have children, or if you just want to do something more, you can find plenty of other types of programs. The following list gives you an idea of some of the other program types that are available:

- Presentation programs   If you ever have to give a presentation, you may want to use a program designed just for creating presentations. You can use this program to create slides, handouts, and notes. Microsoft PowerPoint, Corel Presentations, and Freelance Graphics are popular presentation programs.

Scan through the advertisements for software in a computer magazine to see what types of programs are available.

- Internet programs   If you want to use your computer to hook up to the Internet, you need a browser. The two most popular browsers are Netscape Communicator and Microsoft's Internet Explorer. You can find out more about what you need to connect to the Internet in Part 6.

- Financial programs   In addition to spreadsheet programs, you can also use other types of financial programs. For example, you can purchase a program to keep track of your check register. One of the most popular check management programs is Quicken. You can also find programs for calculating your income tax, managing your small business, handling major accounting tasks, and so on.

- Personal Information Managers   Most people have several things to keep track of: people, events, appointments, places, and so on. Personal Information Managers (or PIMs) are just the program for storing names and addresses, keeping track of your schedule, jotting notes, and so on. You can think of this type of program as your electronic day planner.

- Games and educational software   Two other broad categories of software are games and educational software. Here you find a wealth and variety of programs. Learn how to cook, chart your family tree, play a card game, conquer another planet, learn French. The list goes on and on.

- Desktop publishing programs   If you want utmost control over the printed document, you may want to use—in addition to a word processing program—a desktop publishing program. These programs provide even more control of the layout of the page. Microsoft Publisher is a fairly simple desktop publishing program. PageMaker, on the other hand, is a more robust package.

- Drawing programs   You can use a simple drawing program, such as Paint, which is included with Windows 95 and 98, to create simple illustrations. You can also find more sophisticated programs for drawing and working with images. For instance, Adobe Illustrator andAdobe Photoshop are two such packages.

- Utility programs   When you want to fine-tune your computer, you may want to investigate some of the utility programs that are available. These programs may add capabilities to your system such as virus checking, backing up, and so on.

Cheat Sheet

Checklist for Setting Up a PC

- Do you have a flat surface (usually a desk) for your monitor, keyboard, and mouse?
- If you have a desktop system, do you have a spot for the PC?
- If you have a sound card and speakers, do you have a spot for your speakers?
- Do you have a spot for the printer?
- After all the components are in place, are they close enough to connect to the system unit?
- Do you have enough space to work?
- Do you have a power outlet close by?
- Do you have a surge protector?
- Is the monitor at the proper height and distance?
- Do you have any glare problems with the placement of the monitor?
- If you have a modem and plan on using it to connect to the Internet or other online services, do you have a phone connection nearby?
- Is the keyboard placed so that you can type properly (your wrists should be kept flat as you type)?

5

Setting Up Your PC

If you already have your PC set up, you may want to skim this chapter to see if you can pick up any pointers. If you just purchased a new PC, you can read this chapter to figure out how to set up all the components. The first step is to find a good workspace and that requires a little planning.

Basic Survival

Do You Have Enough Desk Surface?

You need a flat surface (usually a desk) for your monitor, keyboard, and mouse. If you have a desktop system, you also need a spot for the PC. You can stack the monitor on top of the system unit if you want.

If you have a sound card and speakers, you need a spot for your speakers. And finally, don't forget your printer. All these elements are connected to the PC via cables, so they have to be close to the system unit.

If you have a tower system (the system unit sits on the floor), you need to pick a spot for the system unit that is close enough to the desktop items. Remember—everything plugs into the back of the PC.

Don't forget that you also need some space to work. You want some place where you can lay out papers and write on your desk, too.

Is Power Close By?

The system unit, monitor, and printer need to be plugged into an outlet, so you need a power source close by. You might want to purchase a surge protector. Not only can you plug all the components into this power strip, but the surge protector can protect against power surges, which can damage data and your PC.

In severe weather, unplug the entire system from the power and the telephone lines to avoid damage to your PC.

Keep in mind that not all power supplies/surge protectors are the same. A surge protector outlet strip gives you surge protection and has a specific rating for surges. Also, these types usually have a guarantee from the manufacturer that if your equipment is damaged, they will reimburse a "flat" monetary rate. These also can provide protection for a telephone line.

You can also purchase a power conditioning unit, such as an American Power Conversion UPS backup. These not only have a "circuit breaker" to cut the circuit when a large surge is detected, but also provide a DC battery backup when the power is out and allow the computer to continue to operate for a period of time (usually around 15 minutes). Be sure you get one that offers protection against power surges and not just a plain old power supply.

Can You See the Monitor Okay?

Be sure that you can comfortably view the monitor. You don't want the monitor too close or too far. Also, check the height of the monitor. You don't want to strain your neck, so be sure the monitor is at or just below eye level.

Also, if you place the computer in a room with windows, check for glare on the monitor. Remember to check during different times of the day to avoid early morning or late afternoon glare from the sun. You can also purchase anti-glare filters for your monitor.

Beyond Survival

Is a Phone Jack Nearby?

If you have a modem and plan on using it to connect to the Internet or other online services, you need a phone line connection. This is another consideration as you plan where to put your PC. You should also get a surge protector for the phone line or a surge strip with built-in modem protection.

Can You Type Comfortably?

When deciding where to place your keyboard, keep in mind that you want your wrists flat as you type. If you bend them up or down, you can develop a repetitive stress injury such as carpal tunnel syndrome. You can purchase computer desks that have a separate, pull-out shelf for the keyboard. And you can also get keyboard and wrist rests that help with this.

Can You Find Your Books, Disks, and Programs?

You should also find a place to keep your books (manuals, and so on) that is easy to get to. Also, you want to place your program disks in a safe place. They don't have to be within arm's reach, but you may need them again, so put them someplace secure—not wet, hot, or near anything magnetic. Finally, you often copy files from your hard drive to floppy drives. Find some place to keep your data files; these probably do need to be handy.

Cheat Sheet

Turning On the PC

1. Flip (or press) the power switch for the PC.
2. If necessary, press the power switch for the monitor.

Shutting Down the PC

1. Click the Start button in the Windows taskbar.
2. Select the Shut Down command.
3. Select Shut Down.
4. Click the OK button (Windows 98) or the Yes button (Windows 95).

Restarting the PC

1. Click the Start button and select Shut Down.
2. Select Restart.
3. Click the OK button.

6

Turning the PC On and Off

Turning on a PC is as simple as flipping the power switch.
Turning off the PC, however, isn't the same. You need to use a
special command to turn off the PC. And you may get "stuck"
and need to restart your computer.

Basic Survival

Turning On the PC

To use your PC, start by turning on the monitor and printer.
Then you simply turn the PC on. You should see some information flash across screen as your system goes through its startup routine. For instance, you may see the results of a memory
check. You may see setup commands for your hardware. After
the system starts up, you should see Windows 98 (or whatever
operating system you have on your PC).

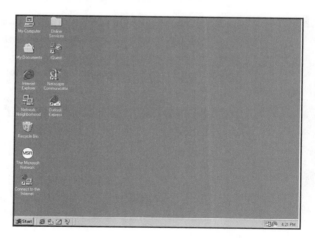

Shutting Down the PC

Windows takes care of all the background details of using your
PC—things such as storing files, handling the printer, and so
on. Because it is often busy in the background, you shouldn't
just turn off your PC. Instead, use the proper shut down procedure so that Windows can take care of any housekeeping tasks
before turning off the power.

Follow these steps to shut off your PC properly:

1. Click the Start button in the Windows taskbar and select Shut Down. You see the Shut Down Windows dialog box.

2. Select Shut down.

3. Click the OK button (Windows 98) or the Yes button (Windows 95).

When you see a message saying that it is safe to turn off your PC, you can turn it off, or your PC may turn off by itself.

Restarting Your PC

If your system won't respond, check the following:

- Check to see whether the disk activity light is blinking. You can find this button on the front of the PC. If the light is blinking or you hear sounds, the PC may be busy saving a file or handling some other activity. Wait a few minutes.

- Be sure you know where you are. It's easy to switch to a different program, say back to the Windows desktop, without intending to. You think you are typing in your word processing program, but you are really back at the desktop, and Windows doesn't understand all that typing. Try clicking in the program window or using the taskbar to make sure you are in the program you think you are.

- Check the screen. As another example, you may have opened a menu or dialog box without realizing it. Again, if you try typing, all you may hear are beeps. Try pressing Esc (the Escape key) to close any open menus or dialog boxes.

If all else fails, you can restart your PC:

1. Click the Start button and select Shut Down. You see the Shut Down Windows dialog box.

2. Select Restart.

3. Click the OK button.

Beyond Survival

What to Do If You Can't Restart from the Start Menu

If you can't click to get the Start menu open, you have to use a different method to restart. Try the keyboard method: Press and hold down the Ctrl key. Then press Alt and Delete. You often see this abbreviated as Ctrl+Alt+Delete. When you press this key combination, you see the Close Program dialog box. Try ending the tasks that are displayed. If nothing happens, try clicking the Shut Down button.

If the keyboard method doesn't work, press the Reset button on the front of the PC. And if that doesn't work or if you don't have a Reset button, try turning the PC off, waiting a minute or so, and then turning it back on.

What to Do If Nothing Happens When You Turn On the PC

If nothing happens when you turn on your PC, check the following:

• Do both the PC and the monitor have power?

• Are all the components connected?

• Did you turn on both the monitor and the PC? They each have separate power buttons.

• Do you need to adjust the monitor? The monitor includes buttons for controlling the brightness of the display. It's easy to think the monitor isn't working when in fact you just can't see anything because of the brightness or other settings. Check these controls.

What to Do If You Don't See the Windows Desktop

More than likely you have Windows 95 or 98 on your PC, but if you don't see the Windows desktop shown in the preceding section, your system may have a different setup.

One possibility is that you have a different operating system. You can refer to your system documentation about how to use the operating system on your PC.

Another possibility is that you have another desktop manager working on top of Windows. I've seen this on some new PCs. The manufacturer adds a layer over Windows (a shell that runs on top of Windows), with its own set of windows and controls and icons for using the PC. Personally, I think this makes using the PC more difficult. Each setup is different, so you can't ask others for help or really use a general-purpose book such as this one. If this is the case, I'd recommend looking in your system documentation and figuring out how to turn off the desktop manager and just use Windows. Usually the shell is loaded from the Startup menu, and you can disable it by removing it from this folder.

Cheat Sheet

Icon   Desktop

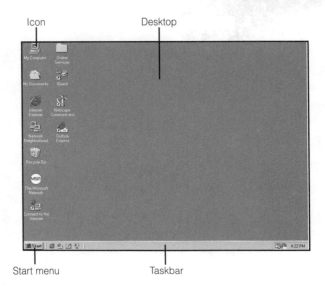

Start menu   Taskbar

7

Understanding the Windows Desktop

When you start your PC, you see the Windows desktop. This is always your starting place, and like your physical desktop, the Windows desktop includes several tools to get you started. Each of these items is placed on the *desktop* (the background area).

Basic Survival

Desktop Icons

You can place different items on the desktop so that they are always available. Each item is represented by a little picture called an icon. (You learn more about adding items to the desktop in Chapter 27, "Creating Shortcuts.") Windows includes several icons by default.

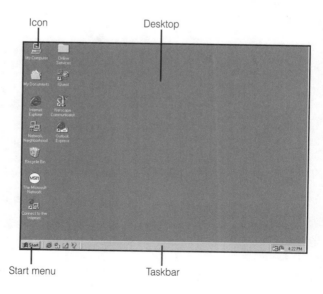

Icon   Desktop

Start menu   Taskbar

The My Computer icon is used to display the contents of your PC. You learn more about using this icon in Chapter 19, "Displaying Files and Folders."

The Recycle Bin icon is used to store files, folders, and programs you have deleted. Chapter 23, "Deleting and Undeleting Files," explains deleting and undeleting files.

You may have several other icons. For instance, if you are hooked up to a network, you may see the Network Neighborhood icon, which you can use to access and display the contents of the network. (Part 7 covers networking.) You may have icons for setting up MSN (Microsoft Network), a folder for online services, or an icon for your Inbox.

You may have icons that you have added yourself. My desktop, for instance, includes icons for programs that I frequently use.

The Start Button

Probably the most important item on the Windows desktop is the Start button. Not only do you use this to start programs, but also to access most Windows features and commands.

To display the Start menu, click the Start button. You see the following choices:

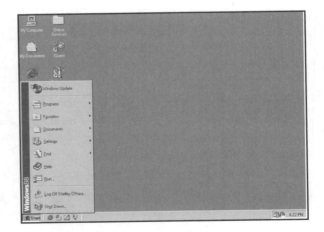

- **Programs** Use this command to start a program. Programs are organized into folders, displayed as submenus on the Programs menu. You learn more about starting programs in Part 2.

- **Favorites** Use this to access a list of folders and Internet Web sites you have added to your list of Favorites.

- **Documents** Use this command to open a document you just recently worked on. This method for starting a program and opening a document is also covered in the next part.

- **Settings** Use this command to access the Control Panel, Taskbar, Start Menu, and Printers folders, which you can use to set up and customize different Windows components. Customizing is the topic of Part 4.

- **Find** Use this computer to search for files or folders on the PC. Finding folders and files is covered in Chapter 25, "Searching for a File or Folder."

- **Help** Use this program to get online help, as covered in Chapter 10, "Getting Help."

- **Run** Use this command to run programs, usually done for installing new programs. You can read about installing programs in Chapter 33, "Installing and Uninstalling Programs."

- **Shut Down** Use this command to shut down the computer before you turn off the power. Chapter 6, "Turning the PC On and Off," explained how to perform this task.

The Taskbar   The Start button is the first item in the *taskbar*, the horizontal bar along the bottom of the desktop. This button also includes buttons for each window you have open or program you have running, which makes it easy for you to see what you have open. More importantly, the taskbar is what you use to switch among different programs.

If you work with more than one program, you may want to switch from one to the other. Windows' taskbar makes it easy. To switch to another program or window, simply click the button for that program or window in the taskbar. That program or window becomes active.

The taskbar also displays the current time and status icons for different tasks such as printing, email, and so on in the far left. Along the right, you see the Quick Launch toolbar (if you have Windows 98 or Internet Explorer 4). You can use this toolbar to get connected to the Internet.

To display the current date, put the mouse pointer on the time.

You can change the placement and look of the taskbar. For more information on these changes, see Chapter 32, "Changing the Taskbar."

Cheat Sheet

Selecting Commands from the Start Menu

1. Click the Start button.

2. To display a submenu, put the pointer over the command you want to select and pause. You can also click the command.

3. Continue selecting commands from submenus by pointing to them until you get to the selection you want.

4. Click your selection.

Selecting Commands in a Program

1. Click the menu you want to open.

2. Click the command.

3. If you see a submenu, click the command you want from this menu.

4. If you see a dialog box, make your selections and click the OK button.

Using a Dialog Box

- **Tab**   Click the tab to see the options for that tab.
- **Text box**   Type the entry in the text box.
- **Spin box**   Type the value in the spin box or use the spin arrows to scroll through the values.
- **List box**   Click the item you want from the list.
- **Drop-down list box**   Click the down arrow to display the list and then click the item you want from this list.
- **Check box**   Click the box to turn on an item (checked) or turn off an option (unchecked).
- **Option button**   Click the button to turn on an item (darkened button) or turn off an option (blank button).
- **Command button**   Click the OK button to confirm your choices. Click Cancel to close the dialog box without carrying out the command.

8

Selecting Commands

Selecting commands is simple. After you learn how to select a
command in one program, you can use these same skills in just
about any program.

Basic Survival

**Selecting
Commands
from the
Start Menu**

To select a command from the Start menu, follow these steps:

1. Click the Start button. You see the top-level menu commands.

2. To display a submenu, put the pointer over the command you want to select and pause. You can also click
the command. W hen the pointer is over a command
with a submenu (indicated with an arrow), the submenu
is displayed. Continue selecting commands from submenus by pointing to them until you get to the selection
you want.

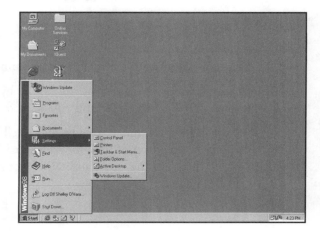

3. Click your selection.

The command is carried out. For instance, if you select a program icon, that program is started.

Selecting Commands in a Program

In most programs, the menu bar appears at the top of the screen. This bar lists the names of the menus, and you can click them to display a list of commands in each menu. To select a command from a program menu, follow these steps:

1. Open the program, and then click the menu you want to open. You see a list of commands (here, you see the File menu from Microsoft Word).

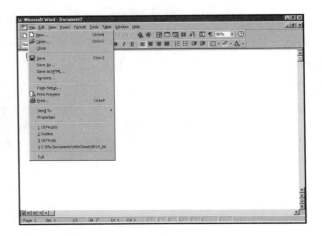

2. Click the command.

For some commands, the command is immediately carried out.

If you select a command that is followed by an arrow, you see a submenu. Click the command you want from this menu.

To close a menu without making a selection, press the Esc key.

If you select a command followed by an ellipsis, you see a dialog box, which prompts you for additional information about how to carry out the command. Make your selections and click the OK button.

Using a Dialog Box

For some commands, the program needs additional information. For instance, when you print a document, you may specify the number of copies to print or the printer to use. In this case, the program displays a dialog box, with the available options for carrying out the command.

Every dialog box is different and contains different options, but they all work in a similar fashion. After you learn the basics of selecting each type of item, you are set. The following figures identify the different types of options, and the list explains how to select each type of option.

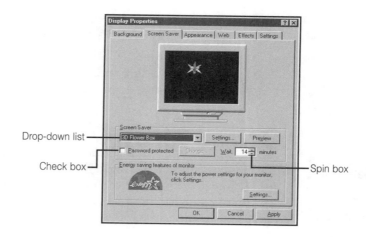

Drop-down list

Check box

Spin box

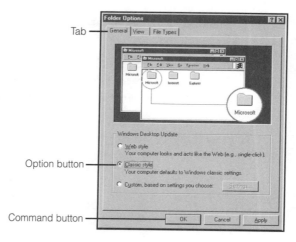

Tab

Option button

Command button

- **Tab**   Click the tab to see the options for that tab.
- **Text box**   Type the entry in the text box.
- **Spin box**   Type the value in the spin box or use the spin arrows to scroll through the values.
- **List box**   Click the item you want from the list.
- **Drop-down list box**   Click the down arrow to display the list and then click the item you want from this list.
- **Check box**   Click the box to turn on an item (checked) or turn off an option (unchecked).
- **Option button**   Click the button to turn on an item (darkened button) or turn off an option (blank button).
- **Command button**   Click the OK button to confirm your choices. Click Cancel to close the dialog box without carrying out the command.

Beyond Survival

Selecting a Program Command from the Keyboard

If you prefer, you can use the keyboard to select a menu command. Some commands have shortcut keys; you can press this key or key combination to select the command. You can also open a menu and select a command using the keyboard. Follow these steps:

1. Open the program, and then press the Alt key to activate the menu bar.

2. Press the "key" letter of the menu. The key letter is underlined onscreen. For instance, press F to open the File menu. (You often see steps 1 and 2 listed as press Alt+F.)

3. Press the "key" letter for the command.

Using a Shortcut Menu

In addition to the main commands, you can often use shortcut menus. You can display these menus and select commands by using the right mouse button. Follow these steps:

1. **Point to the item you want to work with.** In Windows, you can display a shortcut menu for the desktop, the taskbar, icons, files, the time in the status bar, and other "hot" spots. You can also use shortcuts in other programs by clicking the item or object you want to modify.

2. **Click the right mouse button.** A shortcut menu is displayed. (Here, you see the shortcut menu for the desktop.)

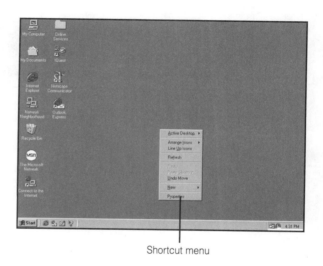

Shortcut menu

3. **Click the command you want.**

Cheat Sheet

Maximize button

Title bar   Minimize button   Close button

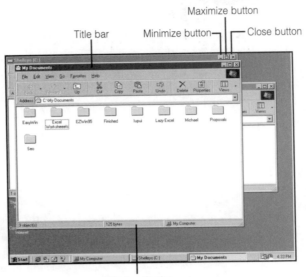

Window border

9

Working with Windows

Everything in Windows is displayed in a window, and one of the key skills you need to learn is how to manipulate a window—that is, how to open, close, resize, and move a window.

Basic Survival

Opening a Window

Some windows display the contents of a disk or folder. For instance, the My Computer icon displays the contents of your system and the Recycle Bin icon displays the contents of the Recycle Bin folder. To open this type of window, double-click the icon. The window is displayed on the desktop, and you also see a button for the window in the taskbar.

Some windows display a program. To open this type of window, start the program. The program is started and displayed in a program window, and Windows adds a button for this program to the taskbar.

Both types of windows have the same set of controls.

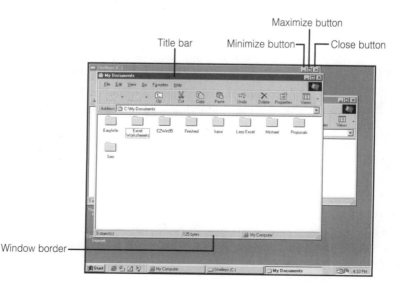

Maximize button

Title bar   Minimize button   Close button

Window border

One thing that can be confusing for beginners is that when you are working in a program, you actually have two windows open: the program window and the document window. Each has its own set of controls. The set in the title bar controls the program window. The set below this one (to the far right of the menu bar when the document window is maximized) controls the document window.

Closing a Window

To close a window, click the Close (X) button in the title bar. If you close a program window, you exit that program. If you have made changes to a file since you last saved it, you are prompted to save the file before the program exits.

You can also close programs or windows by right-clicking the button for that program or window on the taskbar. From the shortcut menu, select the Close command.

Beyond Survival

Resizing a Window

You may have several windows open at the same time. To view them all, you may need to make some adjustments to the windows' sizes. You have a lot of options for resizing. You can use the buttons in the title bar, or you can drag the window borders. For resizing, do any of the following:

- To minimize a window (shrink it to a button on the taskbar), click the Minimize button. When you minimize a window, that window or program is still running, but is not displayed in a window.

- To maximize a window (expand it to fill the entire screen), click the Maximize button. When a window is maximized, the window does not have borders, so you cannot resize by dragging the border. Also, the Maximize button becomes the Restore button.

- To restore a maximized window to its previous size, click the Restore button.

- To resize a window, put the pointer on any of the window's borders, but not on the title bar. Drag the border to change the size of the window.

Moving a Window

If you have several windows open, you may also need to move windows around to see just what you want. You can move a window by following these steps:

1. Put the pointer on the title bar.

2. Drag the window to the location you want.

Arranging Open Windows

You can have Windows arrange all windows onscreen for you. To do so, follow these steps:

1. Right-click a blank area of the taskbar.

2. Select Cascade, Tile Horizontally, or Tile Vertically.

Cascade displays the windows one on top of another; you can see the title bar of each window (as shown in the following figure). Tile Horizontally displays each window in horizontal panes. Tile Vertically displays each window in vertical panes.

Cascaded windows

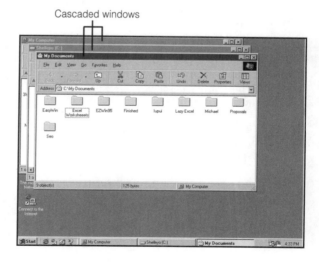

Cheat Sheet

Using Help Contents

1. Click the Start button and select the Help command.
2. If necessary, click the Contents tab.
3. Click any of the book topics until you see the help page you want.
4. Click the help page.
5. When you are finished reading the help information, close the window by clicking the Close button.

Using the Help Index

1. Click the Start button and select the Help command.
2. Click the Index tab.
3. Type the first few letters of the topic for which you want help.
4. Double-click the topic you want.
5. When you finish reading this information, close the window by clicking the Close button.

Searching for a Help Topic

1. Click the Start button and select the Help command.
2. Click the Search tab.
3. In the first text box, type the word or words that you want to find.
4. Click the List Topics button.
5. Double-click the topic you want.
6. When you finish reading this information, close the window by clicking the Close button.

10

Getting Help

You really can't be expected to remember each command and feature of Windows. You find that you remember the day-to-day stuff, the tasks you perform all the time. But for less often used tasks, you may need a little reminder. You can use online help for these tasks.

Basic Survival

**Using Help
Contents**

You can use online help to look up a topic in one of three ways: using the table of contents, using the index, or searching for a topic.

If you have Windows 95, online help works a little differently. The basic methods are the same, but the help window looks different.

Follow these steps to look up a topic in the table of contents:

1. Click the Start button and select the Help command. The Windows Help dialog box appears.

2. If necessary, click the Contents tab. Windows displays the Contents tab, which contains a list of topics, each represented by a book icon. You can open any of these topics.

3. Click any of the book topics. (Note that you single-click in Windows 98.) Windows displays additional subtopics. Do this until you see a help "page." Help pages are indicated with question mark icons.

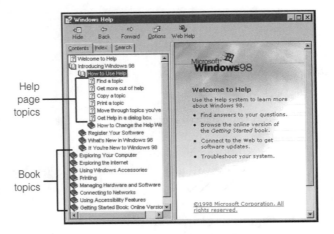

Help page topics

Book topics

4. Click the help page. (You single-click in Windows 98.) The help information appears in the right part of the window.

Help topics   Help information

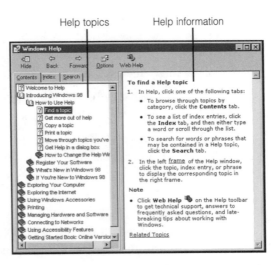

5. When you are finished reading the help information, close the window by clicking the Close button.

Using the Help Index

If you can't find the topic in the table of contents, you also can try looking up a topic using the index. Follow these steps:

1. Click the Start button and select the Help command.

2. Click the Index tab.

3. Type the first few letters of the topic for which you want help. Windows displays matching topics in the list box.

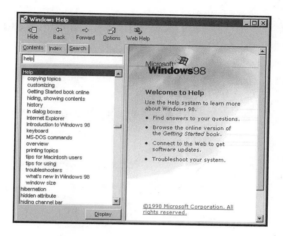

4. Double-click the topic you want. You see the appropriate help information.

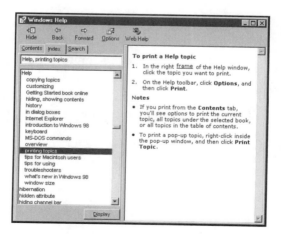

5. When you finish reading this information, close the window by clicking the Close button.

Beyond Survival

Searching for a Help Topic

If you can't find a topic by browsing the table of contents or looking it up in the index, you can search for a topic. Follow these steps:

1. Click the Start button and select the Help command.

2. Click the Search tab.

3. In the first text box, type the word or words that you want to find.

4. Click the List Topics button. Windows displays matching topics in the list box.

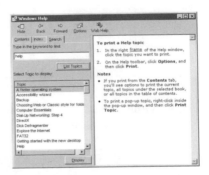

If this is the first time you've used Search, the Find Setup Wizard appears. Click Next, then Finish. The Wizard creates a wordlist for searching.

5. Double-click the topic you want. You see the help information for this topic.

6. When you finish reading this information, close the window by clicking the Close button.

PART

2

Program Basics

You buy a computer so that you can use it to do things, and you do things by using an application. The best thing about Windows programs is that most programs operate in a similar fashion. After you learn a few key tasks, such as saving a document, you can use these skills in any Windows program. This part covers the skills you can use in most any type of application. The following topics are covered:

- Starting a Program
- Switching Among Programs
- Using Windows Programs
- Selecting Text
- Copying, Cutting, and Pasting Text
- Saving a Document
- Opening and Closing a Document
- Printing a Document

Cheat Sheet

Starting a Program from the Start Menu

1. Click the Start menu and select Programs.
2. If necessary, select the program folder(s).
3. Click the program icon to start the program.

Starting a Program from a Shortcut Icon

1. Double-click the shortcut icon.

Starting a Program and Opening a Document

1. Click the Start button.
2. Select the Documents command.
3. Click the document you want to open.

Starting a Program with the Run Command

1. Click the Start button.
2. Select the Run command.
3. In the Open text box, type the program name, including the complete path to the program.
4. Click the OK button.

11

Starting a Program

Most of your time spent using Windows involves using some
type of application. The easiest way to start a program is by
using the Start menu. After you get more proficient, you might
want to investigate some shortcuts for starting programs.

Basic Survival

**Starting a
Program**

The Start menu lists all the programs you have on your system.
These programs are organized into folders. To start a program,
open the folder that contains the program name and icon.
Follow these steps:

1. Click the Start menu and select Programs. You see a list
of the program folders and icons on your system.

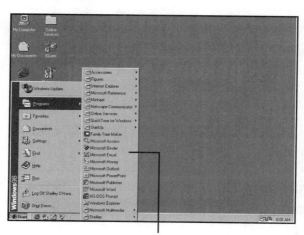

Click the program to start.

2. If you see the program name and icon, click it to start
the program.

If the program is stored in a folder, point to the folder.
Do this until you see the program icon. Click the icon to
start the program.

Beyond Survival

Starting a Program and Opening a Document

If you want to open both a document and start a program, you can use the Documents command. Windows keeps track of the last 15 documents you worked on. You can open any of these documents (and at the same time start that program) by following these steps:

1. Click the Start button.

2. Select the Documents command. You see a list of documents you have recently worked on.

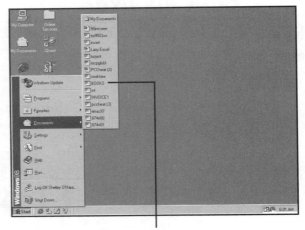

Click the document to open.

3. Click the document you want to open. Windows starts the program and opens the selected document.

Starting a Program with a Shortcut Icon

For programs you use all the time, you may want to put a shortcut to that program on the desktop. You can simply double-click the shortcut icon to start the program.

Follow these steps to create a shortcut icon:

1. In Windows Explorer or My Computer, select the program for which you want to create a shortcut. Be sure that you can see at least part of the desktop. (For more help on displaying files, see Chapter 19, "Displaying Files and Folders.")

2. With the right mouse button, drag the icon from the window to the desktop.

3. From the shortcut menu that appears, select Create Shortcut(s) Here. Windows adds the shortcut icon to the desktop.

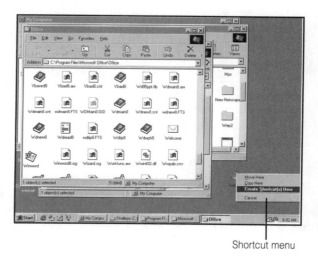

Shortcut menu

The shortcut is not the actual file, but it links to the file. You can delete the shortcut by right-clicking it and selecting Delete. The original program, file, or folder is not affected.

Using the Run Command

You can also use the Run command to start a program. To use this command, you need to know the name of the program as well as the path of folders where this program is stored. Usually Run is used to install new programs (see Chapter 33). Follow these steps to use the Run command:

1. Click the Start button.

2. Select the Run command. You see the Run dialog box.

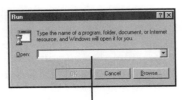

Type the program name.

3. In the Open text box, type the program name. Be sure to include the complete path to the program. If you are not sure where the program is stored, you can use the Browse button to browse through the folders on your system and find the file you want.

4. Click the OK button.

The program is started. For instance, if you use the Run command to start an installation program, you see that installation program. Follow the onscreen prompts to install the program.

Starting a Program Each Time You Start Windows

As a final method, you can also put programs in your Startup folder. Each time you start Windows, all programs in the Startup folder are started. Follow these steps:

1. Right-click the Start button and select Explore.

2. In the pane on the left, display the program icon for the program you want to add to your Startup folder.

3. In the right pane, double-click the Programs folder and then double-click the StartUp folder.

4. Drag the program file from the pane on the left to the StartUp folder on the right.

5. Click the Close button.

Each time you start Windows, this program is started.

To remove a program from the StartUp folder, right-click the Start button and select Explore. Then double-click the Programs folder and double-click the StartUp folder. Right-click the icon you want to delete and select the Delete command.

Cheat Sheet

Switching Among Open Programs

1. Click the taskbar button for the program you want.

Switching Among Open Programs Using the Keyboard

1. Press Alt+Tab until you highlight the program you want.

12

Switching Among Programs

Another useful feature in Windows is the capability to run more than one program at a time. You can then switch from program to program. For instance, if you are typing a report in a word processing program, you can switch to your spreadsheet program to review (and even copy data from) sales data.

Basic Survival

Switching Among Programs

Windows displays a button in the taskbar for each window that is open and program that is running. The button for the current program (or window) appears depressed. To switch to a different program, click the taskbar button for that program.

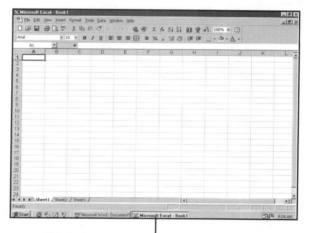

Click the button to switch to that program or window.

Beyond Survival

Using the Keyboard to Switch

If you used Windows 3.1, you might be accustomed to switching programs by using a key combination. You can also switch to a different program in Windows 95 or 98 by using the same key combination. Follow these steps:

1. Hold down the Alt key and press Tab. You see a toolbar with icons for each program that is running.

2. Continue to hold down the Alt key, and press Tab until the program you want is boxed. When you release the keys, Windows switches to that program.

Cheat Sheet

WordPad   A mini-word processing program.

Paint   A simple drawing program.

Notepad   A text editor.

Calculator   An onscreen calculator.

Solitaire   A card game.

Windows Explorer   A file management program.

MS-DOS prompt   A program to access and run DOS commands.

Entertainment folder   Programs for playing sounds, CDs, and movies.

System Tools folder   Programs for system maintenance (see Part 5).

Communications folder   Programs for getting connected to the Internet (see Part 6).

13

Using Windows Programs

When you get a new system, you might not even know what you have and what you don't. It's confusing for beginners to get a new PC and wonder "where did I get that?" For instance, Windows comes with several useful programs. You can review this section to help get a clue about what programs your system contains.

Basic Survival

Windows Programs

Windows 95 and 98 include several different programs that are set up when Windows is installed. You can expect to find the following programs:

- *Accessory programs*   You can find these programs in the Accessories folder on the Programs menu. Expect to find folders for Games; Multimedia programs (CD Player, Media Player, Sound Recorder, Volume Control); and System Tools (programs for backing up your system, defragmenting your hard drive, and so on). You also have icons for these programs: Calculator, Dial-Up Networking, HyperTerminal, Notepad, Paint, Phone Dialer, and WordPad.

- *MS-DOS prompt*   Use this program to access the MS-DOS prompt for working with files, installing DOS programs, and doing other DOS tasks.

- *Windows Explorer*   Use this program to work with the files on your system.

- *Control Panel programs*   You find these programs by clicking the Start button, selecting Settings, and then selecting Control Panel. You learn more about these tools for customizing Windows in Part 4.

Depending on how Windows was installed, it is possible that a few of these programs may not have been set up. You can add Windows components, as covered in Chapter 33.

You start these programs as you do any other. Click the Start menu, select Programs, select the program folder (if necessary), and then click the program name.

Beyond Survival

Using WordPad

WordPad is a mini-word processing program. If your word processing needs are fairly simple, you can use this program to create documents. It provides some basic editing and formatting features.

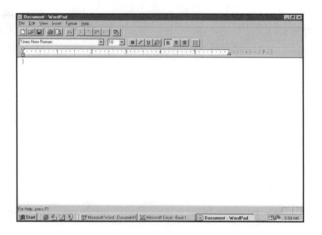

Using Paint

If you like to draw or just want to play around, try the simple drawing program included with Windows. This program, called Paint, also lets you open and sometimes modify other graphic files.

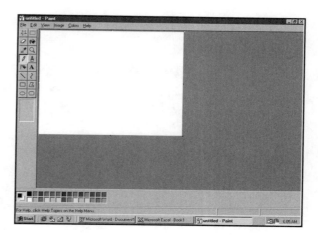

Using Calculator

The program I probably use most often (next to Solitaire!) is the Calculator. When you need to figure a simple calculation, start Calculator. You can use the mouse or the keyboard to enter your calculation.

Playing Solitaire

Windows also includes some games, such as Solitaire. Playing games can be more than entertainment, too. Playing Solitaire is a good way to get the hang of using the mouse, for instance.

Typing a DOS Command

You can use the DOS prompt to type a command or run a DOS program. Follow these steps:

1. Click the Start button and select Programs.

2. Select MS-DOS prompt. You see a DOS window.

3. Type your command and press Enter.

4. To close the window, click the Close (X) button or type **EXIT** and press Enter.

Using Other Programs

You can expect to find three types of programs on your computer: Windows programs, preinstalled programs (those that came with the computer), and programs that you have installed yourself. This chapter mentions most of the Windows programs.

In addition, your system may have come with some software as part of the purchase. What you received varies depending on not only the manufacturer of your PC, but also the model you purchased. For instance, if you purchased a "family" PC, you may have received some entertainment and home software (encyclopedia, games, and so on). If you purchased a "business" PC, you may have received some business software such as Microsoft Office. Usually this software comes preinstalled.

Your computer also contains any programs that you have installed yourself. You can find more information on setting up new programs in Chapter 33.

Cheat Sheet

Selecting Text with the Mouse

1. Click at the start of the text you want to select.
2. Hold down the mouse button and drag across the text.
3. Release the mouse button. The text appears in reverse video.

Selecting Text with the Keyboard

1. Move the insertion point to the start of the text you want to select.
2. Hold down the Shift key.
3. Use the arrow keys to highlight the text you want to select.

Selecting a Range in a Worksheet

1. Click the first cell you want to select.
2. Hold down the mouse button and drag across the other cells you want to select.
3. Release the mouse button.

Selecting an Object

1. Click the object.

14

Selecting Text

Although this book can't tell you how to use each of the applications you have on your PC, it can teach you some key skills used in many programs. The most common skill is probably selecting something (text, numbers, and objects). When you want to work with text or an object, you start by selecting it. If you want to make text bold, you first select the text. If you want to chart a set of figures, you select the data to chart. If you want to copy an object you've drawn, you select that object. Selecting is the first step for many editing and formatting tasks.

Basic Survival

Selecting Text

To select text, follow these steps:

1. Click at the start of the text you want to select.

2. Hold down the mouse button and drag across the text.

3. Release the mouse button. The text appears in reverse video.

Selected text

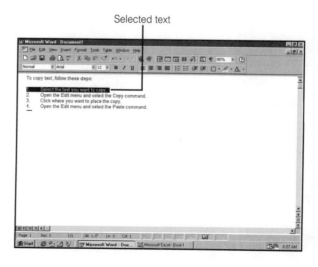

After the text is selected, you can then perform the editing or formatting task. To deselect text, click outside it.

Beyond Survival

Selecting Text with the Keyboard

If you prefer to keep your hands on the keyboard, you can use it to select text. Follow these steps:

1. Move the insertion point to the start of the text.

2. Hold down the Shift key.

3. Use the arrow keys to highlight the text you want to select.

Selecting a Range in a Worksheet

In a spreadsheet program, you follow a similar procedure for selecting a set of cells (called a *range*). For instance, you might want to select a set of cells to total. Follow these steps:

1. Click the first cell you want to select, in one corner of the range.

2. Hold down the mouse button and drag across the other cells you want to select, to the opposite corner.

To select a graphic image, click it once.

3. Release the mouse button.

Cheat Sheet

Deleting Text

1. Select the text you want to delete.
2. Press the Delete key.

Moving Text

1. Select the item you want to move. To select text or a range in a worksheet, drag across it. To select a graphic object, click it.
2. Click the Cut button on the toolbar, or open the Edit menu and select the Cut command.
3. Move the mouse to where you want to paste the text. Click once so that the cursor is in the correct place.
4. Click the Paste button on the toolbar, or open the Edit menu and select the Paste command.

Copying Text

1. Select the item you want to copy.
2. Click the Copy button on the toolbar, or open the Edit menu and select the Copy command.
3. Move the mouse to where you want to place the copy. Click once so that the cursor is in the correct place.
4. Click the Paste button on the toolbar, or open the Edit menu and select the Paste command.

15

Copying, Cutting, and Pasting Text

One of the greatest benefits of an electronic document is that the data is not yet committed to paper. Therefore, you can easily make editing changes. You can delete text you don't need, move text to a different location, or copy text you want to reuse.

If your program includes a toolbar, look for buttons for cutting, copying, and pasting.

Windows programs use the metaphor of scissors and paste for these editing tasks. You first "cut" the text you want to move or copy and then "paste" the text to its new location. You can find these commands in the Edit menu of most programs. The process for moving and copying text is similar from program to program.

Basic Survival

Deleting Text

To delete text, follow these steps:

1. Select the text you want to delete.

2. Press the Delete key. The other text is adjusted to fill in the gap.

Moving Text

To move text, follow these steps:

1. Select the item you want to move. To select text or a range in a worksheet, drag across it. To select a graphic object, click it.

Text selected to be moved

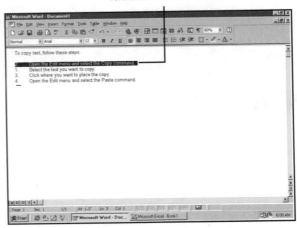

2. Click the Cut button on the toolbar, or open the Edit menu and select the Cut command.

3. Move the mouse to where you want to paste the text. Click once so that the cursor is in the correct place.

4. Click the Paste button on the toolbar, or open the Edit menu and select the Paste command.

Text moved to a new spot in the document

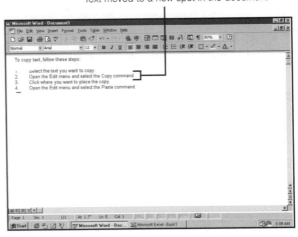

The text is pasted to the new location.

Copying Text

Copying text is similar to moving, but you have two copies of the selected text: one in the original spot and one where you paste the copy. Follow these steps:

1. Select the item you want to copy.

2. Click the Copy button on the toolbar, or open the Edit menu and select the Copy command.

Text selected to be copied

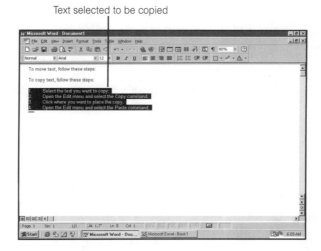

3. Move the mouse to where you want to place the copy. Click once so that the cursor is in the correct place.

4. Click the Paste button on the toolbar, or open the Edit menu and select the Paste command.

Text copied to a new location

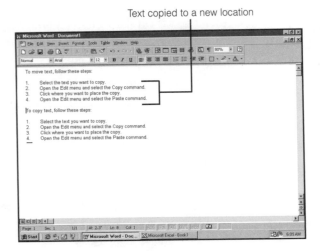

The text is pasted to the new location. You now have two copies of the text.

Beyond Survival

Copying to Another Program

You can also copy data from one program to another. If you simply copy and paste, the data is pasted in the receiving program in an acceptable format. For instance, if you copy Excel data to a Word document, it is pasted as a table. You can also insert the data as an object (like a mini-document from the program). You can then edit the inserted object by using the original program.

Follow these steps to copy data to another program:

1. Select the item you want to copy.

2. Click the Copy button, or open the Edit menu and select the Copy command.

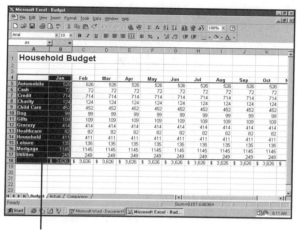

Range selected to be copied

3. Switch to the program where you want to paste the data. (Remember, use the taskbar buttons to switch between programs.)

4. Click the location where you want to paste the data in the document.

5. To simply paste the data, click the Paste button, or open the Edit menu and select the Paste command.

To paste the data as an object, open the Edit menu and select the Paste Special command. Select the format for the data and click OK.

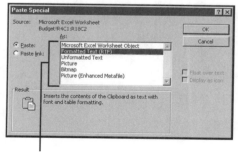

Select how to paste the item.

The data is pasted to the new program (here, as an Excel object in a Word document).

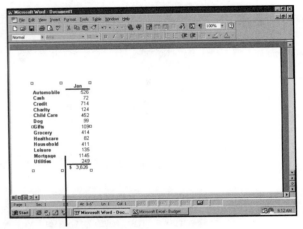

Excel object pasted in a Word document

Cheat Sheet

Saving a Document the First Time

1. Open the File menu and select the Save command.
2. Select a drive from the Save in drop-down list.
3. Select a folder from the folders listed. You can use the Up One Level button to move up one folder in the folder structure.
4. Type a filename.
5. Click the Save button.

Saving a Document Again

1. Open the File menu and select the Save command.

Saving a Document with Another Name

1. Open the File menu and select the Save As command.
2. To save the file on another drive, select a drive from the Save in drop-down list.
3. To save the file in another folder, select a folder from the folders listed. You can use the Up One Level button to move up one folder in the folder structure.
4. Type a new filename.
5. Click the Save button.

16

Saving a Document

One of the most important things you can learn about using a PC is to *save your work*. There's nothing more frustrating than spending hours getting every word in a document just perfect and then having some accident happen before you've saved. If the power goes off, if your system crashes, if you turn off the PC without saving—all that work is lost. You should get in the habit of saving your work and saving often.

Basic Survival

Saving a Document the First Time

When you save a document the first time, you do two things. First, you select a location for the file—a folder on your hard disk where the file is stored. Second, you enter a name. You can enter up to 255 characters, including spaces for a name if you are using Windows 95 or 98. (Previous versions of Windows limited you to an 8-character name.) Use something descriptive, but don't go overboard.

You can type up to 255 characters for a filename, including spaces.

Again, the procedure for saving a document is similar from application to application. The following steps use Microsoft Word as an example. In your program, you may find other features and options for saving, but the general process is the same.

Follow these steps to save a document:

1. Open the File menu and select the Save command. You see the Save As dialog box.

Select a drive from this list.   Up One Level button

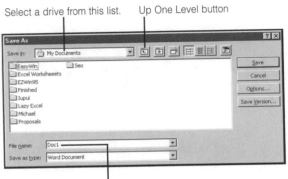

Type a filename here.

Look for a
Save button
in the toolbar
as a shortcut
for selecting
the File, Save
command.

2. Select a drive from the Save in drop-down list.

3. Select a folder from the folders listed. You can use the Up
One Level button to move up one folder in the folder
structure.

4. Type a filename in the File name text box.

5. Click the Save button. The document is saved, and the
name you used appears in the title bar of the document
window.

**Saving a
Document
Again**

After you've saved the document once, you don't have to reenter
the folder and filename. You can simply select File, Save to save
the document to the same folder and with the same name.

Beyond Survival

**Saving a
Document
with
Another
Name**

You can change the name and folder for a document using the
Save As command. You can also use this command to save a
copy of a file. The original remains intact, and you also create a
new file with the new name. Follow these steps:

1. Open the File menu and select the Save As command.
You see the Save As dialog box. The original name and
folder are listed.

2. To save the file on another drive, select a drive from the Save in drop-down list.

3. To save the file in another folder, select a folder from the folders listed. You can use the Up One Level button to move up one folder in the folder structure.

4. Type a new filename.

5. Click the Save button.

Saving a Document As Another File Type

Occasionally, you may need to share files with someone who does not use the same program you do. Most programs enable you to save a file in several different formats. For instance, if you have Microsoft Word (a word processing program), you can save a document as a Word file, a plain text file, a formatted text file, and several other choices. Follow these steps to save a document as another file type:

1. Open the File menu and select the Save As command. You see the Save As dialog box. The original name and folder are listed.

2. To save the file on another drive, select a drive from the Save in drop-down list.

3. To save the file in another folder, select a folder from the folders listed. You can use the Up One Level button to move up one folder in the folder structure.

4. To save the file with a different name, type a new filename.

5. Display the Save as type drop-down list and select the appropriate file type.

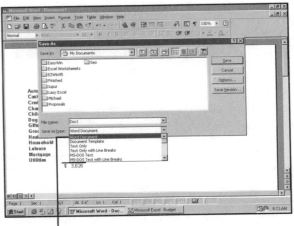

Select the file format.

6. Click the Save button.

Cheat Sheet

Opening a Document

1. Open the File menu and select the Open command.
2. If necessary, change to the drive and folder that contains the file you want to open. You can use the Look in drop-down list to select a different drive. Use the Up One Level button to move up a level in the folder structure.
3. When you see your file listed, double-click it.

Closing a Document

To close a document, do any of the following:

- Open the File menu and select the Close command.
- Click the Close (X) button for the *document* window. Be sure you click the button for the document window and not the program window.
- Press Ctrl+F4.

Creating a New Document

1. Open the File menu and select the New command.
2. If you see a dialog box listing templates, select the one you want and click the OK button.

17

Opening and Closing a Document

The purpose of saving a document is so that you can open it again. You may want to open a document so that you can use it again, or perhaps you weren't finished and need to make additional editing or formatting changes. You can also create a new, blank document.

Basic Survival

Opening a Document

When you want to work on a document you've saved previously, use the File, Open command. Follow these steps:

1. Open the File menu and select the Open command. You see the Open dialog box. The following shows the Open dialog box for Microsoft Word. The dialog box may look a little different for other programs.

Select the drive.   Click to move up one level in the folder structure.

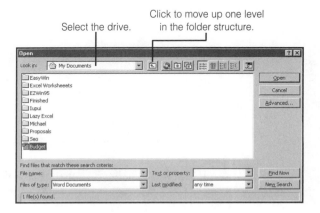

2. If necessary, change to the drive and folder that contains the file you want to open. You can use the Look in drop-down list to select a different drive. Use the Up One Level button to move up a level in the folder structure.

3. When you see your file listed, double-click it.

Closing a Document

After you save, the document remains open onscreen. You can continue working. If you are finished with the document, you can close it (to save resources). To close a document, do any of the following:

As a shortcut, look for an Open button in the program toolbar.

- Open the File menu and select the Close command.

- Click the Close (X) button for the *document* window (in the title bar of the document window). Be sure you click the button for the document window and not the program window.

- Press Ctrl+F4.

Creating a New Document

When you start most programs, you see a blank document onscreen. You can start typing away. What do you do when you want a new "sheet of paper"? Create a new document:

1. Open the File menu and select the New command. You may be prompted to select a template for the new document.

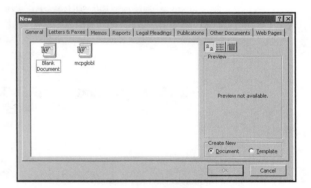

2. If you see a dialog box listing templates, select the one you want and click the OK button.

As a shortcut, look for a New button in the pro- gram toolbar.

A template is a predefined document that can contain text and formatting. For instance, a memo template includes all the headings for a memo (to, from, and so on). Depending on the program, you may find different templates available for your use.

Beyond Survival

Switching Among Open Documents

Just as you can have more than one program running, in most Windows programs, you can work in more than one document. You might copy data, for instance, from one document to another. While writing, you might have your outline open in one document and the current chapter in another. To open another document, simply use File, Open.

To switch among open documents, follow these steps:

1. Open the Window menu. You see a list of all open docu- ments at the bottom of the menu. The current document is indicated with a check mark.

Click the document you want to view.

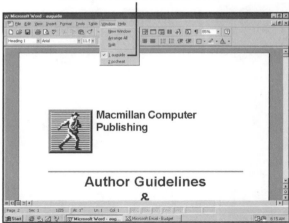

2. Click the document you want. That document becomes the active document.

Displaying All Open Documents

In addition to being able to switch among documents, many programs provide commands for arranging all open documents. The options vary, but the basic process is the same. Follow these steps:

1. Open the Window menu. Look for a command named Arrange, Arrange All, or something similar.

2. Select the command for arranging windows.

Cheat Sheet

Printing a Document

1. Open the File menu and select the Print command.
2. Make any changes to the print options.
3. Click the OK button.

Previewing a Document

1. Open the File menu and select the Print Preview command.

Set Up a Document

1. Open the File menu and select the Page Setup command.
2. Make your selections.
3. Click the OK button.

18

Printing a Document

Most documents are created with the intent of being printed and possibly distributed. If your printer is connected, printing is as easy as selecting a command or toolbar button. If your printer is not set up, refer to Chapter 37, "Setting Up a Printer" in Part 4 of this book. And if you are printing on a network, check out Part 7.

Basic Survival

Printing a Document

Look for a Print button as a shortcut for printing, or use the keyboard shortcut Ctrl+P.

You can print in most programs using the File, Print command. What may be different is the options you can select for printing. You may be able to select the printer to use, the number of copies to print, what to print, and more. You make these selections in the Print dialog box. Follow these steps to print a document:

1. Open the File menu and select the Print command. Most programs display a Print dialog box where you can select such printing options as what to print and the number of copies to print.

Select the printer.

Select the number of copies to print.

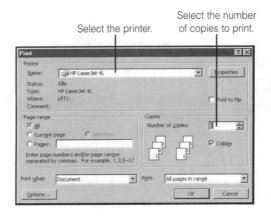

2. Make any changes to the options.

3. Click the OK button.

Beyond Survival

Previewing a Document

Most programs enable you to preview a document before print-ing. Doing so lets you get a sense of how the document prints on the page. You can then make any changes (such as adjust the margins) *before* you print.

To preview a document, look for a Print Preview command in the File menu. The following shows a preview of a document in Word.

Use the toolbar to make changes.

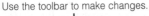

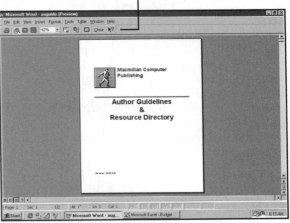

Setting Up a Document Page

Want to change the margins? Add a header or footer? Most programs provide formatting features for changing the look of the page. For content changes, look in the Format menu. For page changes, try the File, Page Setup command. The following shows some of the available options for setting up a page in Microsoft Word.

Click a tab to see other options.

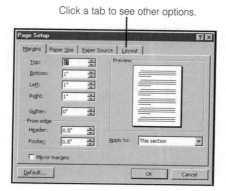

Make your selections in the dialog box and then click the OK button.

PART

3

File Basics

After you start using a computer, you'll be surprised how quickly the files pile up. You have document files, program files, and other types of files. To keep your computer organized, you need to set up folders and store similar files together. You should also periodically delete files you don't need and back up important files. This part covers all the key file management tasks, including the following:

- Displaying Files and Folders
- Creating and Working with Folders
- Selecting Files
- Moving and Copying Files
- Deleting and Undeleting Files
- Renaming Files and Folders
- Searching for a File or Folder
- Displaying File, Folder, Disk, and System Properties

Cheat Sheet

Using My Computer to Display Files and Folders

1. Double-click the My Computer icon on your desktop.
2. Double-click the drive you want to open, and then double-click the folder you want to open.
3. Continue double-clicking folders until you find the folder or file you want to work with.
4. To close a window, click the Close button.

Changing the View

1. In the file window, open the View menu.
2. Select the view you want: Large Icons, Small Icons, List, or Details.

Sorting the Contents

1. In the file window you want to sort, open the View menu and select the Arrange Icons command.
2. From the submenu, choose the sort order you want.

Using Windows Explorer to View Files and Folders

1. Click the Start button.
2. Select Programs and then Windows Explorer.
3. To expand a folder (see the subfolders within), click the plus sign (+) next to the folder. To collapse the folder and hide these subfolders, click the minus (–)sign.
4. To view the contents of a drive or folder, click the item on the left side.

Working in Web View

1. Click the Start button.
2. Select Settings and then Folder Options.
3. Select Web style and click OK.

19

Displaying Files and Folders

The most common analogy used to describe files, folders, and hard disks is that of a filing cabinet. You can think of your hard disk as one big filing cabinet. If all your files were lumped together on the hard disk, finding the file you needed would be difficult, if not impossible. Instead, much like a filing cabinet has file folders, a hard disk can be divided into folders. You can then store similar files together in a folder. A folder can contain files or other folders.

The folders you have on your system vary. Usually programs are installed in their own folder, so you probably have a folder for each program on your system. That folder may contain other folders for different parts of the program. Windows 98, for instance, has its own folder with many subfolders for different items. In addition to the folders already set up on your system, you can create your own folders, as covered later in this part.

When you want to view the folders and files on your system, you can use My Computer. You can then work with the displayed items, as covered in later chapters in this part. If you prefer, you can also use Windows Explorer, also covered here.

Basic Survival

Using My Computer to Display Files

You can use My Computer to browse through the drives and folders on your system. The contents of each drive or folder are displayed in a separate window. Most novices prefer this method. Follow these steps:

1. Double-click the My Computer icon on your desktop. You see icons for each drive on your system, as well as some system folders.

Drives

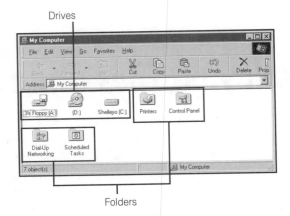

Folders

2. Double-click the drive you want to open.

3. Double-click the folder you want to open.

4. Continue double-clicking folders until you find the folder or file you want to work with. Notice that the taskbar displays a button for each open window.

Click this button to close the window.

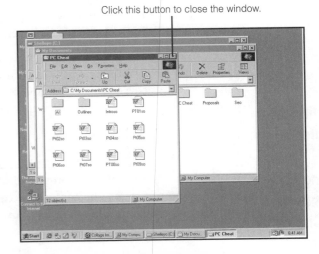

5. To close a window, click the Close button.

Changing the View

Most of the time, the contents of a file window are displayed as large icons. You can also select to view them as small icons, as a list, or as a detailed list with file dates and sizes. Follow these steps to try another view:

1. In the file window, open the View menu. You see a list of different view options.

2. Select the view you want: Large Icons, Small Icons, List, or Details. The contents are displayed in that view. The following shows a Details view of a file window.

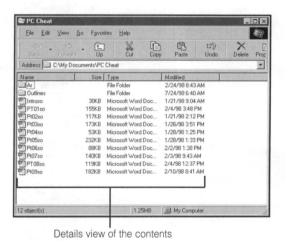

Details view of the contents

Shortcut: Use the Views button in the toolbar to change views.

Keep in mind that this change affects only the current window.

Beyond Survival

Sorting the Contents

You can sort the contents of a window so that you can more easily find the files you want. Windows enables you to arrange the files in a folder by name, type, date, and size. Sorting the files is even easier if you choose to view them by the file details first. In this view, you can simply click the column heading to sort the files by that heading (that is, click Size to sort by size).

Follow these steps:

1. Open the window you want to sort and change to the view you want.

2. Open the View menu and select the Arrange Icons command.

109

3. From the submenu, choose the sort order you want. Windows sorts the files in the selected order. The following shows a detailed view of a file window sorted by date modified.

Contents sorted by this column

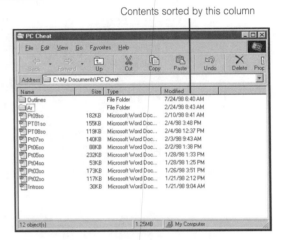

Using Windows Explorer

You can also use Windows Explorer to work with files and folders. This program presents your system contents in a hierarchical structure in a two-column window. The left pane displays all the drives and folders on your system. The right pane displays the contents of the selected drive or folder from the left. Because you can see the entire system in one window, some users prefer this method to using My Computer. You can try both and see which you prefer. Follow these steps to start Windows Explorer:

1. Click the Start button.

2. Select Programs and then Windows Explorer. The program is started, and you see the contents of your system in a hierarchical view.

Click a minus sign to collapse. Current drive and folder Contents of current drive and folder

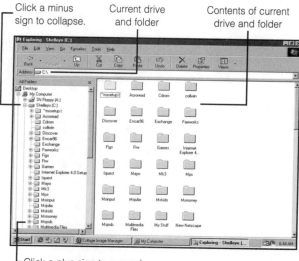

Click a plus sign to expand.

3. To expand a folder (see the subfolders within), click the plus sign (+) next to the folder. To collapse the folder and hide these subfolders, click the minus (–)sign.

4. To view the contents of a drive or folder, click the item on the left side. The right side shows the contents of that selected item.

Working in Web View

New with Windows 98 is the capability to browse the contents of your system, much like browsing a Web page. Rather than double-clicking to open an icon, you can simply click once. (This book assumes that you are *not* working in Web view.) Follow these steps to use this view:

1. Click the Start button.

2. Select Settings and then Folder Options. You see the General tab of the Folder Options dialog box.

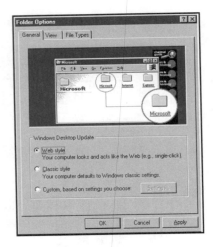

3. Select Web style and click the OK button. The contents of your system are displayed as links. You can click the icon to open it.

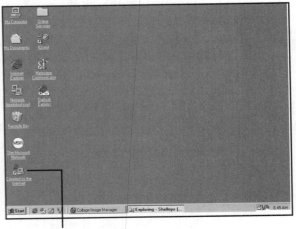

Single-click an icon to open it.

You can use Active Desktop to view Web content on your desktop. You can also browse channels of Internet content from the Channel bar. For information on Active Desktop as well as using the Channel bar, see Part 4 of this book.

Cheat Sheet

Creating a New Folder

1. Open the drive or folder where you want to place the new folder.
2. Open the File menu and select the New command.
3. In the submenu that appears, select Folder.
4. Type a name for the new folder and press Enter.

Deleting a Folder

1. Right-click the folder and select the Delete command.
2. Click the Yes button to confirm the deletion.

Moving Folders

1. Start Windows Explorer.
2. In the right pane, display the folder you want to move.
3. In the left pane, display the folder or drive where you want to move the folder.
4. Drag the folder to the new location.

Copying Folders

1. Start Windows Explorer.
2. In the right pane, display the folder you want to copy.
3. In the left pane, display the folder or drive where you want to place the copy.
4. Hold down the Ctrl key and then drag the folder you want to copy to the location where you want to place the copy.

20

Creating and Working with Folders

To keep your files organized, you should create folders for your data files. The organization and names for your folders are up to you. You might want to use the My Documents folder and set up subfolders for different program types (Word documents, Excel worksheets, and so on). Or you might set up folders for each project or each person that uses your PC. You can select the method that you prefer.

Basic Survival

Creating a New Folder

To create a new folder, follow these steps:

1. Open the drive or folder where you want to place the new folder. You can open the folder using My Computer or select the folder in the Windows Explorer window.

2. Open the File menu and select the New command. In the submenu that appears, select Folder. Windows adds a new folder (named New Folder) to the window. The name is highlighted so that you can type a more descriptive name.

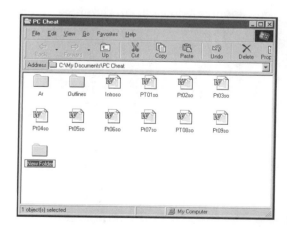

3. Type a name for the new folder and press Enter. The folder is added.

Deleting a Folder

If you create a folder that you no longer need, you can delete it. Windows deletes the folder and all its contents. Follow these steps:

Check the folder contents before you delete it.

1. Right-click the folder by using either My Computer or Windows Explorer.

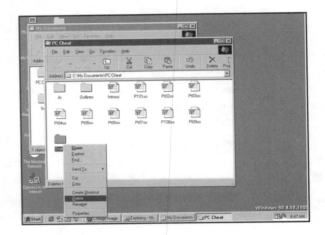

2. Select the Delete command.

3. Click the Yes button to confirm the deletion. The folder and all its contents are deleted.

If you make a mistake, you can undo the deletion by using the Edit, Undo command. You can also retrieve the item from the Recycle Bin as covered in Chapter 23, "Deleting and Undeleting Files."

Beyond Survival

Moving Folders

As you work with your computer more and more, you may need to do some reorganizing. For instance, you may set up new folders and want to move existing folders (and their contents) around. You can move a folder by using My Computer or

Windows Explorer, but Windows Explorer is the best tool because you can simply drag the folder from its current location to the new one. Follow these steps:

1. Display the folder you want to move. Remember that you click a folder on the left to display its contents in the pane on the right. Also, you can expand the folder listing by clicking the plus (+) sign next to any of the listed folders.

If the folders are close to each other, you can display them both in the left pane. (If they are far apart in the overall list, you can display the folder you want to move on the right side and then drag to the left.)

2. In the left pane, display the folder or drive where you want to move the folder. You can simply expand and/or scroll the list to display the folder or drive you want.

Folder you want to move to

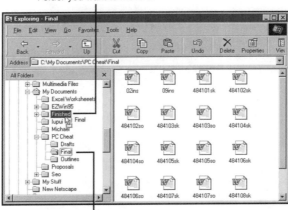

Folder you want to move

3. Drag the folder to the new location. The folder and its contents are moved.

If the results aren't what you expected, choose Edit, Undo and perform the steps again.

Copying Folders

You can make a copy of a folder and all its contents. For instance, you might want to copy an important folder so that you have a backup copy. (For more information on backing up, see Part 5 of this book.) It's easier to copy a folder by using Windows Explorer, so start Windows Explorer and then follow these steps:

1. In the right pane, display the folder you want to copy.

2. In the left pane, display the folder or drive where you want to place the copy. You can simply expand and/or scroll the list to display the folder or drive you want.

3. Hold down the Ctrl key and then drag the folder you want to copy to the location where you want to place the copy. The folder and its contents are copied.

Cheat Sheet

Selecting a File

1. Click the file.

Deselecting a File

1. Click outside the file(s).

Selecting Several Files

To select multiple files, you can do any of the following:

- To select all folders and files in a folder, click the folder, and then open the Edit menu and choose Select All.
- To select files next to each other, click the first file. Then hold down the Shift key and click the last file.
- To select files that are not next to each other, press and hold down the Ctrl key and then click each file you want to select.

21

Selecting Files

The last chapter covered how to work with folders, but you may also want to work with individual files or groups of files. For instance, you may want to delete a group of files or copy a file from a folder to a floppy disk. The first step when working with files is to select the files you want, as covered in this chapter. You can select a single file or a group of files.

Basic Survival

Selecting a File

To select a single file, click it. The file is selected.

This file is selected.

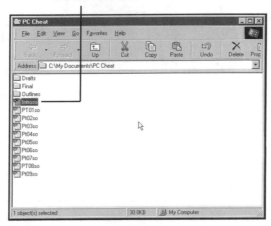

To deselect a file, click outside the file.

Selecting Several Files

For other tasks, you may want to work with several files. For instance, you may want to back up all the files in a folder. To select multiple files, you can do any of the following:

- To select all folders and files in a folder, click the folder, and then open the Edit menu and choose Select All.

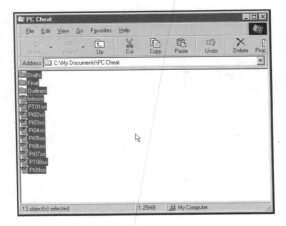

- To select files next to each other, click the first file. Then hold down the Shift key and click the last file. All files in between the two are selected.

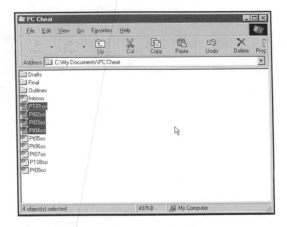

- To select files that are not next to each other, press and hold down the Ctrl key and then click each file you want to select.

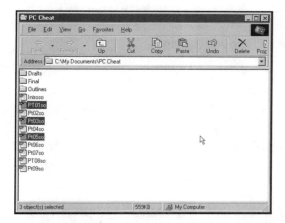

Beyond Survival

Inverting a Selection

You can invert a selection: Select all files that are unselected and deselect all selected files. To do this, open the Edit menu and select the Invert Selection command.

Cheat Sheet

Moving Files by Dragging

1. Start Windows Explorer.
2. In the right pane, display the files you want to move.
3. Scroll the left pane until you see the folder to which you want to move the file(s).
4. Select the file(s) you want to move.
5. Hold down the mouse button and drag the files to the new folder in the left pane of the window.

Copying Files from One Folder to Another

1. Start Windows Explorer.
2. In the right pane, display the files you want to copy.
3. Scroll the left pane until you can see the drive or folder in which you want to place the copies.
4. Select the file(s) you want to copy.
5. Hold down the Ctrl key and drag the selected file(s) to the drive or folder where you want to place the copy.

Copying Files from Your Hard Disk to a Floppy Disk

1. Insert the floppy disk into the drive.
2. Display the files you want to copy by using either My Computer or Windows Explorer.
3. Select the file(s) you want to copy.
4. Right-click the file(s).
5. From the shortcut menu, select Send To and then select your floppy drive (usually A: drive).

22

Moving and Copying Files

When keeping your files organized, you may need to move a file or files from one location to another. You may decide to use a different organization. Maybe you inadvertently saved a document in the wrong folder, or perhaps your projects have grown so much that you need to reorganize your files and put them in different folders.

Copying is similar to moving, but instead of one version of the selected file, you end up with two. For instance, you might need to copy all the files in a folder so that you have extra copies in case something happens to the originals. You might want to copy a file to a floppy disk so that you can take the file with you.

The easiest way to move and copy files is to use Windows Explorer. This program works better than My Computer because you can drag and drop the file all in one window. You can also use a command method, covered later in this chapter.

Basic Survival

Moving Files

To move a file or group of files from one folder to another, follow these steps:

1. Start Windows Explorer.

2. In the right pane, display the files you want to move.

3. Scroll the left pane until you see the folder to which you want to move the file(s).

4. Select the file(s) you want to move.

Folder to move to   Selected files

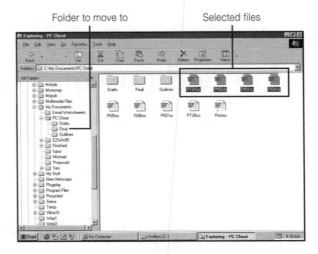

5. Hold down the mouse button and drag the files to the new folder in the left pane of the window. The files are moved.

If you make a mistake, you can undo the move by choosing the Edit, Undo command.

Copying Files from One Folder to Another

Moving files deletes the selected files from one folder or drive and then copies them to another folder or drive. In some cases, you may want to have two copies of the files (that is, leave the files in the original location and copy them to another drive or folder).

To copy from one folder to another by using Windows Explorer, follow these steps:

1. Start Windows Explorer.

2. In the right pane, display the files you want to copy. Select these files.

3. In the left pane, scroll the window until you can see the drive or folder in which you want to place the copies.

4. Hold down the Ctrl key and drag the selected file(s) to the drive or folder where you want to place the copy. You can tell that you are copying because the mouse pointer displays a plus sign.

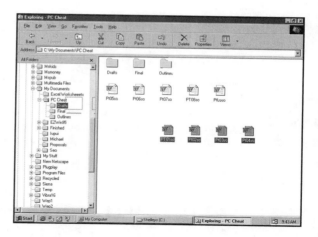

The files are copied to the selected drive or folder.

Copying Files from Your Hard Disk to a Floppy Disk

The easiest way to copy files from your hard disk to a floppy disk is to use the Send To command. Follow these steps:

1. Insert the floppy disk into the drive.

2. Display the files you want to copy by using either My Computer or Windows Explorer.

3. Select the file(s) you want to copy.

4. Right-click the file(s).

5. From the shortcut menu, select Send To and then select your floppy drive (usually Drive A).

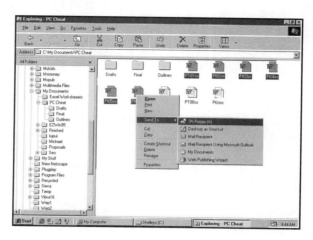

The files are copied to the floppy drive.

Beyond Survival

Moving Files with a Command

Some users can't get the hang of dragging and dropping to copy or move a folder. Also, some may not like working in Windows Explorer. If this is the case, you can use a menu command to move files from one folder to another. Follow these steps:

1. In My Computer or Windows Explorer, select the file(s) you want to move.

2. Open the Edit menu and select the Cut command.

Shortcut: Use the Cut and Paste buttons in the toolbar.

3. Open the folder where you want to place the files.

4. Open the Edit menu and select the Paste command. The selected file(s) are moved to the new folder.

Copying Files with a Command

Just as you can move files with a command, you can also copy them. Again, you may prefer this method to the drag-and-drop method used with Windows Explorer. Follow these steps:

1. In My Computer or Windows Explorer, select the file(s) you want to copy.

2. Open the Edit menu and select the Copy command.

Shortcut: Use the Copy and Paste buttons in the toolbar.

3. Open the folder where you want to place the copied files.

4. Open the Edit menu and select the Paste command. The selected file(s) are copied to the new folder.

Cheat Sheet

Deleting a File

1. Using either My Computer or Windows Explorer, select the file(s) you want to delete.
2. Right-click the selected item(s) and then select the Delete command.
3. When prompted to confirm the deletion, click the Yes button.

Retrieving a Deleted Item from the Recycle Bin

1. On the desktop, double-click the Recycle Bin.
2. Select the items you want to undelete.
3. Right-click the selected items and then select the Restore command.

Emptying the Recycle Bin

1. Double-click the Recycle Bin icon. Check out the contents and be sure the Recycle Bin does not contain any files or folders you want to keep.
2. Open the File menu and select the Empty Recycle Bin command.
3. Confirm the deletion by clicking the Yes button.

23

Deleting and Undeleting Files

As you use your computer more and more, the files you have multiply and eventually you have to weed out the old stuff. Deleting files you don't need frees up the disk space for new files.

When you delete a file or folder, keep in mind that Windows does not really delete the file, but simply moves it to the Recycle Bin. You can undo the deletion and recover the item from the Recycle Bin if you make a mistake and delete a file you need. If you want to permanently get rid of the file, empty the Recycle Bin. This chapter covers all these tasks.

You can also clean up unnecessary files using the Disk Cleanup feature, as covered in Chapter 40, "Defragmenting Your Hard Drive."

Basic Survival

Deleting a File

Follow these steps to delete a file or group of files:

1. Using either My Computer or Windows Explorer, select the file(s) you want to delete.

2. Right-click the selected item(s) and then select the Delete command.

3. When prompted to confirm the deletion, click the Yes button.

The file is deleted. If you make a mistake, you can undo the deletion by using Edit, Undo. You can also retrieve the item from the Recycle Bin, covered next.

Shortcuts:
Click the Delete button in the toolbar or press the Delete key on the keyboard.

Undeleting a File

To retrieve a file from the Recycle Bin and put it back in its original location, follow these steps:

1. On the desktop, double-click the Recycle Bin. You see the contents of this system folder.

2. Select the items you want to undelete.

3. Right-click the selected items and then select the Restore command.

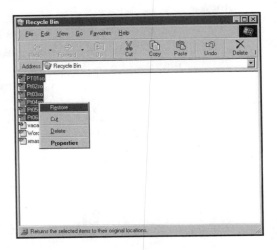

The items are returned to the original folder.

Beyond Survival

Emptying the Recycle Bin

As mentioned previously, files and folders aren't really deleted with the Delete command. They are simply moved to the Recycle Bin, a temporary holding spot. To free up the disk space and really get rid of the files, you must empty the Recycle Bin. Follow these steps:

1. Double-click the Recycle Bin icon. Check out the contents and be sure it does not contain any files or folders you want to keep. After you empty the Recycle Bin, you can't get the contents back.

2. When you are sure you don't need any of the contents, open the File menu and select the Empty Recycle Bin command.

3. Confirm the deletion by clicking the Yes button.

All the files and folders in the Recycle Bin are permanently deleted.

Cheat Sheet

Renaming a File

1. In Windows Explorer or My Computer, display the file you want to rename.
2. Right-click the file and select Rename.
3. Type the new name and press Enter.

Renaming a Folder

1. Right-click the folder you want to rename.
2. Select the Rename command.
3. Type the new name and press Enter.

24

Renaming Files and Folders

When you save a file or create a folder, you assign a name. If this name doesn't work—for instance, the filename isn't easy to remember—you can make a change. You can use up to 255 characters, including spaces. You cannot use any of the following characters:

\ ? : * " < > |

In some DOS and Windows applications, the folder name is truncated to the old 8-character limitation. When a program truncates a folder or filename, it adds a tilde (~) to indicate that the name has been shortened. For instance, if you have the filename **My Reports.doc**, it is shortened to **myrepor~.doc**.

Basic Survival

Renaming a File

Follow these steps to rename a file:

1. In Windows Explorer or My Computer, display the file you want to rename.

2. Right-click the file and select Rename from the shortcut menu that appears. Windows highlights the current name and displays a box around it.

3. Type the new name and press Enter.

Renaming a Folder

If you don't like the name you used when you first created a folder, you can change it. You can type up to 255 characters, including spaces. To rename a folder, follow these steps:

1. Right-click the folder you want to rename. (You can display the folder by using either My Computer or Windows Explorer.)

2. Select the Rename command. The name is highlighted so that you can type a new name or edit the existing name.

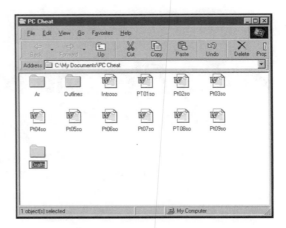

3. Type the new name and press Enter.

Cheat Sheet

Searching for a File or Folder by Name

1. Click the Start button, choose the Find command, and then choose Files or Folders.
2. Type the name of the file or folder you want to search for in the Named text box.
3. To look on a different drive than the one listed, display the Look in list box and select the drive you want to search.
4. If you don't want to look in the subfolders, uncheck the Include subfolders check box.
5. Click the Find Now button.

Searching for a File or Folder by Content

1. Click the Start button, choose the Find command, and then choose Files or Folders.
2. In the Containing text area, type the text you want to find.
3. To change the drive on which Windows conducts the search, display the Look in list box and choose the drive you want to search.
4. Click the Find Now button.

Finding Files and Folders by Date

1. Click the Start button, choose the Find command, and then choose Files or Folders.
2. Click the Date tab, and then click the Find all files option button.
3. Display the drop-down list next to Find all files and select to find all files modified, created, or accessed within the date range.
4. Select the date range.
5. Click the Find Now button.

25

Searching for a File or Folder

After you've worked for months with your applications, your computer becomes filled with various folders and files, which can make it nearly impossible for you to know where everything is. Luckily, Windows includes a command that helps you locate specific files or folders. If you know the name, you can search by name. You can also search for a file by its contents or date.

Basic Survival

Searching for a File or Folder by Name

If you know the name of the file or folder, but just can't remember where you placed it, you can search for the file by name (or partial name). Follow these steps:

1. Click the Start button, choose the Find command, and then choose Files or Folders.

2. Type the name of the file or folder you want to search for in the Named text box. You can use the characters * and ? (known as *wildcards*) in the search. For example, to find all files ending with the extension .doc, type *.**doc**. Similarly, you could type **chap??.*** to find all files beginning with chap, followed by any two characters, and ending in any extension.

Filename to match

Drive to look on

3. To look on a different drive than the one listed, display the Look in list box and select the drive you want to search.

4. Windows looks in the selected drive and all subfolders on that drive. If you don't want to look in the subfolders, uncheck the Include subfolders check box.

5. Click the Find Now button. Windows displays a list of found files and folders at the bottom of the dialog box. You can double-click any of the listed files or folders to go to that file or folder.

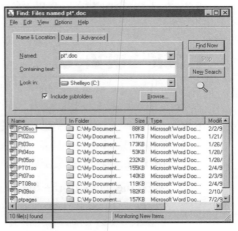

Double-click any file to open it.

If you want to try a new search, you can clear the existing search entries by clicking the New Search button. Confirm that you want to clear the current search by clicking the OK button in the dialog box that appears.

Beyond Survival

Searching for a File or Folder by Content

If you don't know the name of the file or folder you want, but you have some idea of what it contains, you can search for it by content. Pick a unique word or phrase so that you don't end up with too many matches. Follow these steps:

1. Click the Start button, choose the Find command, and then choose Files or Folders.

2. If you want, enter the name of the file you want to search for. You can search on more than one criterion—a filename and content, for instance. If you don't want to limit the search, leave the Named text box blank.

3. In the Containing text area, type the text you want to find.

Text you want to find ——

4. To change the drive on which Windows conducts the search, display the Look in list box and choose the drive you want to search.

5. Click the Find Now button. Windows searches the selected drive and displays a list of found files at the bottom of the dialog box. You can double-click any of the listed files or folders to go to that file or folder.

Finding Files and Folders by Date

As another search possibility, you can search for files within a particular date range. For instance, suppose that you know you worked on a file this past week, but you can't remember the name. You can display a list of all files worked on with a certain date range. Follow these steps:

1. Click the Start button, choose the Find command, and then choose Files or Folders.

2. If you want to search for both a name and date range, enter the name of the file you want to search for in the Named text box. Leave this blank if you don't want to limit the search.

3. Click the Date tab.

4. Click the Find all files option button. Notice that these options then become available.

5. Display the drop-down list next to Find all files and select to find all files modified, created, or accessed within the date range.

6. Select the date range. You can select the between option, and then enter two dates. You can also select an option that specifies the number of months or days. The following shows a search for all files modified during the previous day.

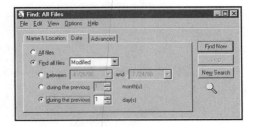

7. Click the Find Now button. Windows searches the selected drive and displays all matching files and folders.

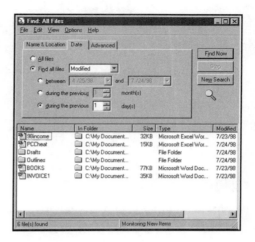

Cheat Sheet

Displaying File or Folder Properties

1. Display the file or folder for which you want information.
2. Right-click the file or folder, and choose Properties from the shortcut menu.
3. Review the information.
4. Click the OK button.

Displaying Disk Properties

1. Open My Computer to display the drives on your system.
2. Right-click the drive and choose Properties from the shortcut menu.
3. Review the information.
4. Click the OK button.

Viewing System Properties

1. Right-click the My Computer icon.
2. Select Properties from the shortcut menu.
3. Review the information.
4. Click the OK button.

Displaying File, Folder, Disk, and System Properties

Shortcut:
Select the
file or folder
and click the
Properties
button in the
toolbar.

Sometimes you may see a file or folder on your system and not know how it got there. What does the file contain? When was it saved to your hard disk? You can get information about the file or folder by viewing its properties. You can also view properties about your hard disk, such as how much space is left. For more detailed information, you can view the properties of your system.

Basic Survival

Displaying File Properties

When you want detailed information about a particular file, including the type of file, location where it is stored, size, and creation, modification, and access dates, view the file properties. Follow these steps:

1. In My Computer or Windows Explorer, display the file for which you want information.

2. Right-click the file and choose Properties from the shortcut menu.

3. Review any of the information. Depending on the file type, you may see different tabs. You can click any of the tabs to view that information.

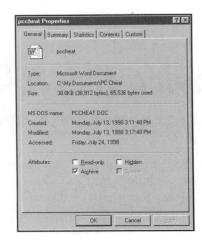

4. Click the OK button.

Displaying Folder Properties

A folder property dialog box is similar to a file property dialog box, but you see the number of files and folders that the folder contains. You also see only the creation date. Follow these steps to view a folder's properties:

1. In My Computer or Windows Explorer, display the folder for which you want information.

2. Right-click the folder and choose Properties from the shortcut menu.

3. Review the information.

4. Click the OK button.

Displaying Disk Properties

You can display a disk's properties when you want to see the size of the disk and how much free space you have. Use this command also to access disk tools (covered in Part 5 of this book). Follow these steps:

1. In My Computer or Windows Explorer, display the drives on your system. (If you want to view the properties of a floppy disk, insert that disk.)

2. Right-click the drive and choose Properties from the shortcut menu.

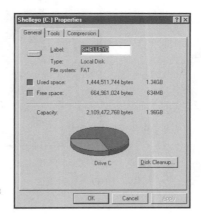

3. Review the information on the General tab.

4. Click the OK button.

Beyond Survival

Viewing System Properties

System properties display some high-tech information about your system, such as devices that are set up and hardware profiles. You may need to review this information if you are troubleshooting a problem such as a device that is not working properly. (See Chapter 45, "Troubleshooting Problems" for more information on troubleshooting problems.) Another reason to view this information is to see which version of Windows you are running. That information is displayed on the General tab. To view system properties, follow these steps:

1. Right-click the My Computer icon on the desktop.

2. Select Properties from the shortcut menu.

3. Review any of the information.

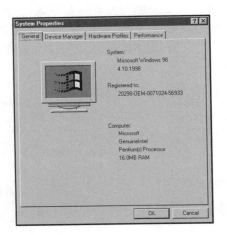

4. Click the OK button.

PART

4

Setup and Customization

You can tinker with the settings of your computer so that it is set up how you like it. Some changes are purely personal. You might add a wallpaper image, for instance, because you *like* it. Other changes may help speed your work. For instance, you can create shortcut icons to the programs, folders, or files you use most often. Still other changes are needed when you add something new to your system—such as a printer or a new program. This part covers features for setting up and customizing your computer. The following topics are covered:

- Creating Shortcuts
- Setting Up the Start Menu
- Changing How the Desktop Looks
- Using a Screen Saver
- Viewing Web Content on Your Desktop
- Changing the Taskbar
- Installing and Uninstalling Programs
- Changing the System Date and Time
- Changing How the Mouse Works
- Playing Sounds and Music
- Setting Up a Printer

Cheat Sheet

Creating a Shortcut

1. In Windows Explorer or My Computer, select the program, file, or folder for which you want to create a shortcut.
2. With the right mouse button, drag the icon from the window to the desktop.
3. From the shortcut menu, select Create Shortcut(s) Here.

Using a Shortcut

- Double-click a folder shortcut to see the contents of that folder.
- Double-click a file shortcut to open that file.
- Double-click a program shortcut to start the program.

Renaming a Shortcut Icon

1. Right-click the icon.
2. Select the Rename command.
3. Type a new name and press Enter.

Deleting a Shortcut Icon

1. Right-click the icon.
2. Select the Delete command.

27

Creating Shortcuts

In your work, you may find that there's one program, folder, or file you use all the time. For quick access to a program, file, or folder, you can create a shortcut to it and place the shortcut on the desktop. You can use this shortcut icon to access the item.

Basic Survival

Creating a Shortcut

The hardest part about creating an icon is finding the actual file, program, or folder that you want to create the shortcut to. After it is displayed, creating the shortcut is simply a matter of dragging and dropping it to the desktop. If you need help with finding or displaying files, see Part 3, "File Basics," which covers these tasks.

Follow these steps to create a shortcut:

1. In Windows Explorer or My Computer, select the program, file, or folder for which you want to create a shortcut. Be sure that you can see at least part of the desktop.

2. With the right mouse button, drag the icon from the window to the desktop.

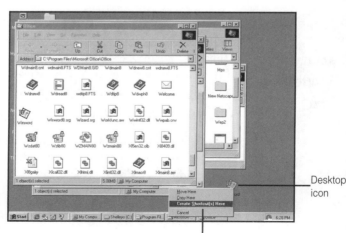

Desktop icon

Shortcut menu

3. From the shortcut menu, select Create Shortcut(s) Here. Windows adds the shortcut to the desktop. In this example, you see a shortcut icon to Microsoft Word for Windows (Winword) added to the desktop.

Shortcut icon added
to desktop

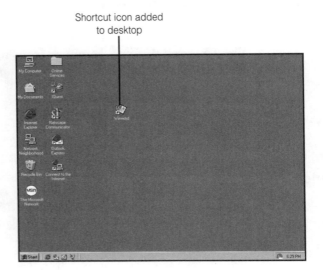

**Using a
Shortcut**

After the shortcut is added to the desktop, you simply double-click the icon to access the folder, file, or program. If you double-click a folder shortcut, you see the contents of that folder. When you double-click a file shortcut, that file is opened. Double-click a program shortcut to start the program.

Beyond Survival

**Renaming a
Shortcut
Icon**

When you create a shortcut icon, Windows displays the name of the file below the icon. You may prefer a different name. You can easily rename a shortcut icon by following these steps:

1. Right-click the icon.

2. Select the Rename command. The current name is selected so that you can type a new name or edit the existing name.

152

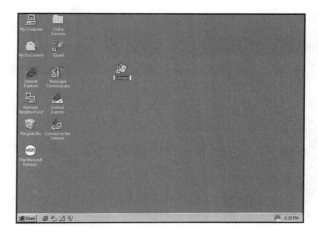

3. Type a new name and press Enter.

Deleting a Shortcut Icon

The shortcut icon on your desktop is not the actual file or pro-gram, but it is a pointer to it. You can delete the shortcut icon if you don't need it. For instance, your desktop may become cluttered with all kinds of icons. If you don't use them, delete them so that your desktop is neat and tidy. Follow these steps to delete a shortcut icon:

1. Right-click the icon.

2. Select the Delete command.

To move an icon, drag it to another spot on the desktop and release the mouse button.

The icon is removed from the desktop. The original program, file, or folder is not affected. If you want to delete the program from your hard disk, uninstall it as covered in Chapter 33, "Installing and Uninstalling Programs."

153

Cheat Sheet

Adding Programs to the Start Menu

1. Open the Start menu, select the Settings command, and select Taskbar & Start Menu.
2. Click the Start Menu Programs tab.
3. Click the Add button.
4. Enter the command line for the program you want to add. Or click the Browse button and select the program by browsing through the folders on your system.
5. Click the Next button.
6. Select the folder in which you want to place the program and click the Next button.
7. Enter a name in the text box or accept the one Windows displays. Click the Finish button to add the new program.

Deleting Programs on the Start Menu

1. Open the Start menu, select the Settings command, and select Taskbar & Start Menu.
2. Click the Start Menu Programs tab.
3. Click the Remove button.
4. Display the program you want to remove. To do so, you may need to expand the folder listings. Click the plus sign next to the folder that contains your program.
5. Select the program you want to remove.
6. Click the Remove button.
7. Click the Close button to close this dialog box.
8. Click the OK button to close the Taskbar Properties dialog box.

28

Setting Up the Start Menu

You can control what items appear on the Start menu. You can add programs, delete programs, add folders, and change where items are placed. You can set up the Start menu so that it is organized how you want it.

Basic Survival

Adding Programs to the Start Menu

When you install a new program, usually the Installation program takes care of adding the program to the Start menu. If it isn't added, you can add it yourself. Follow these steps:

1. Open the Start menu, select the Settings command, and select Taskbar & Start Menu. You see the Taskbar Properties dialog box.

2. Click the Start Menu Programs tab.

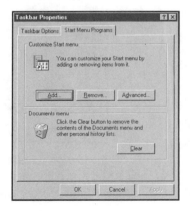

3. Click the Add button. You see the Create Shortcut dialog box.

Type the program
name here.

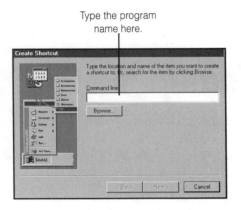

If you don't
know the
program
name, use the
Browse but-
ton to find it.

4. Enter the command line for the program you want to add. Or click the Browse button and select the program by browsing through the folders on your system.

5. Click the Next button. You are prompted to select a folder for the new program.

Select the folder
for the program.

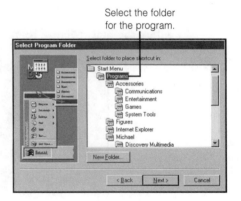

6. Select the folder in which you want to place the program and click the Next button.

To create a new folder, click the New Folder button. Type the name and press Enter.

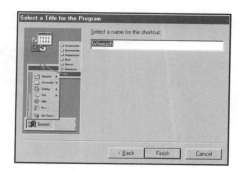

7. Enter a name in the text box or accept the one Windows displays. Click the Finish button to add the new program.

**Deleting
Programs
on the Start
Menu**

If your Start menu becomes cluttered, you may want to delete icons for programs you don't use. At first, you may go a little crazy and add all kinds of icons. Then, after you use the computer more and more, you may want to streamline the Start menu and weed out programs that are not used.

Keep in mind that removing a program from the Start menu does not remove the program and its files from your hard disk. To do this, you can uninstall the program or manually delete the program and its related folders and files. See Chapter 33, "Installing and Uninstalling Programs," in this part.

To remove an item from the Start menu, follow these steps:

1. Open the Start menu, select the Settings command, and select Taskbar & Start Menu. You see the Taskbar Properties dialog box.

2. Click the Start Menu Programs tab.

3. Click the Remove button. You see the Remove Shortcuts/Folder dialog box.

4. Display the program you want to remove. To do so, you may need to expand the folder listings. Click the plus sign next to the folder that contains your program.

Program selected
for removal

5. Select the program you want to remove.

6. Click the Remove button.

7. Click the Close button to close this dialog box.

8. Click the OK button to close the Taskbar Properties dialog box.

Beyond Survival

Adding Folders to the Start Menu

If your Start menu becomes really huge, you might want to organize your programs into folders. Some programs set up folders for themselves when you install the program. Also, Windows sets up some folders. You can also add new folders yourself and move the program icons to the new folder. For instance, you might set up folders by task or program or for each person that uses the PC.

Follow these steps to add a folder:

1. Open the Start menu, select the Settings command, and select Taskbar & Start Menu. You see the Taskbar Properties dialog box.

2. Click the Start Menu Programs tab.

3. Click the Advanced button. You see the Start menu in Windows Explorer.

4. Select the folder in which the new folder should be placed. You may need to expand the list to see the folder.

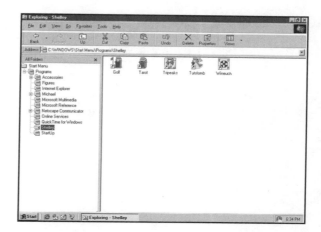

5. Open the File menu, select the New command, and then select Folder.

6. Type a name for the folder and press Enter. The folder is added.

7. Click the Close (X) button.

8. Click the OK button.

Rearranging the Start Menu

After you set up folders, you can organize your Start menu, putting the program icons in the folder and order you want. Rearranging the Start menu is similar to moving or copying files or folders (covered in Part 3, "File Basics"). Follow these steps:

1. Open the Start menu, select the Settings command, and select Taskbar & Start Menu. You see the Taskbar Properties dialog box.

2. Click the Start Menu Programs tab.

3. Click the Advanced button. You see the Start menu in Windows Explorer.

159

4. Click the icon or folder and drag it to the folder where you want it placed. Do this for each program you want to move.

5. Click the Close (X) button.

6. Click the OK button.

Cheat Sheet

Wallpapering Your Desktop

1. Right-click the desktop and select Properties.
2. In the Wallpaper list, select the wallpaper you want to use.
3. Click the OK button.

Using a Pattern for the Desktop

1. Right-click the desktop and select Properties.
2. Click the Pattern button.
3. Click the pattern you want to use.
4. Click the OK button.
5. Click the OK button.

Using a Different Color Scheme

1. Right-click the desktop and select Properties.
2. Click the Appearance tab.
3. Display the Scheme drop-down list box and select the color scheme you want to use.
4. Click the OK button.

Changing How the Icons Are Displayed

1. Right-click the desktop and select Properties.
2. Click the Effects tab.
3. Check any of the visual effects you want to turn on. Uncheck any effects you want to turn off.
4. To change the icon used for a desktop icon, select the icon and then click the Change Icon button. In the Change Icon dialog box, select the icon you want to use and click OK.
5. Click the OK button.

29

Changing How the Desktop Looks

The desktop is the background of the Windows screen. If you don't like the plain desktop background, you can make some changes. You can use wallpaper, display a pattern, change the color scheme, and change how the icons are displayed, as covered in this section. You can also select a different resolution (or screen area).

Adding wallpaper or patterns uses additional memory so if you don't have a lot of memory, or if you notice a drop in performance after adding this element, turn it off.

Basic Survival

Wallpapering Your Desktop Windows comes with several wallpaper designs (BMP files) that it installs in the \WINDOWS folder. You can select from several different wallpaper styles including bubbles, circles, houndstooth, and more. Follow these steps to select a wallpaper for the desktop:

1. Right-click the desktop and select Properties from the shortcut menu that appears. The Display Properties dialog box appears, with the Background tab selected.

2. In the Wallpaper list, select the wallpaper you want to use. You see a preview of how the wallpaper looks on the sample monitor.

View the preview here.

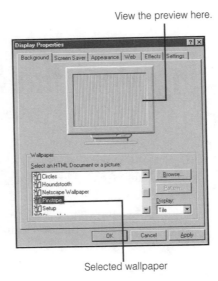

Selected wallpaper

3. If you see only a small image in the center, the image is centered. Open the Display drop-down list and select Tile.

4. When you find the wallpaper you want to use, click the OK button. The wallpaper is added to the desktop.

Select None to turn off wallpaper.

If you change your mind and want to turn off the wallpaper, follow the same steps, but select (None) from the Wallpaper list.

Using a Pattern

If you can't find a wallpaper you like, you can try the patterns. You can use any of several predesigned patterns including bricks, buttons, cargo net, daisies, and others. Note that you can select a pattern or wallpaper, but not both. If you select both, the wallpaper takes precedence.

Follow these steps to add a pattern to the desktop:

1. Right-click the desktop and select Properties from the shortcut menu that appears. The Display Properties dialog box appears, with the Background tab selected.

2. Click the Pattern button. You see the Pattern dialog box.

3. Click the pattern you want to use. You see a preview of the selected pattern.

View the preview here.

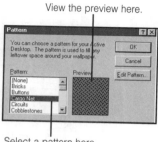

Select a pattern here.

4. When you find the pattern you want, click the OK button.

In the Display Properties dialog box, you see a preview of the selected pattern.

5. Click the OK button to use this pattern.

If you change your mind and want to turn off the pattern, follow the same steps, but select (None) from the Pattern list.

Using a Different Color Scheme

You can also customize the colors used for onscreen elements, including the active title bar, desktop, application background, or menus. The easiest way is to use one of the predefined color schemes. To do so, follow these steps:

1. Right-click the desktop and select Properties from the shortcut menu. The Display Properties dialog box appears.

2. Click the Appearance tab. You see the current scheme as well as how each element appears in this selected scheme.

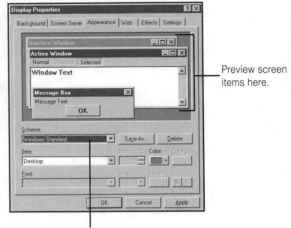

Preview screen items here.

Select a color scheme.

3. Display the Scheme drop-down list box and select the color scheme you want to use. You see a preview of how the desktop looks by using this new scheme.

4. Click the OK button. Windows uses the selected scheme for all onscreen elements.

If you change your mind and want to go back to the original colors, follow the same steps. Select Windows Standard from the Scheme drop-down list.

Changing How the Icons Are Displayed

Another change you can make to how your desktop appears is to change the look of the icons. You can select visual effects such as large icons, animated windows, and other changes. Follow these steps:

1. Right-click the desktop and select Properties from the shortcut menu. The Display Properties dialog box appears.

2. Click the Effects tab.

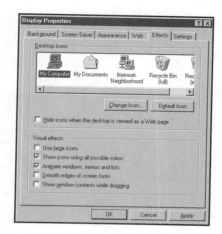

3. Check any of the visual effects you want to turn on. Uncheck any effects you want to turn off.

4. To change the icon used for a desktop icon, select the icon and then click the Change Icon button. In the Change Icon dialog box, select the icon you want to use and click OK.

5. Click the OK button. Windows makes the changes to the desktop icons.

If you change your mind and want to go back to the original icon, follow the same steps. Select the icon you want to change and click the Default Icon button.

Changing the Screen Area

If you want to change the number of colors used in your display or the size of the screen area, follow these steps:

1. Right-click the desktop and select Properties from the shortcut menu. The Display Properties dialog box appears.

2. Click the Settings tab.

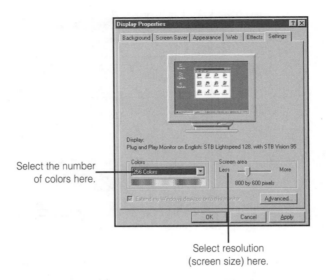

Select the number of colors here.

Select resolution (screen size) here.

3. Display the Colors drop-down list and select the number of colors to use for the display.

4. To change the screen area, drag the screen area slider bar left or right to make the size of the items (resolution) larger or smaller. The preview shows how your screen looks with the currently selected settings.

5. Click the OK button.

6. When prompted, click OK. You see how the screen looks using the new settings, and Windows prompts you to confirm the change.

7. Click the Yes button. Windows makes the changes.

Beyond Survival

Using Another File for the Wallpaper

You aren't limited to the wallpaper files included with Windows. You can use other graphic file types as the wallpaper image. You can select, for instance, an image from the Web to use as your wallpaper. Follow these steps:

1. Right-click the desktop and select Properties from the shortcut menu that appears. The Display Properties dialog box appears, with the Background tab selected.

2. Click the Browse button. You see the Browse dialog box, which displays all background file types.

Up One Level button

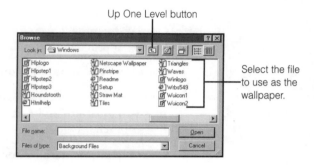

Select the file to use as the wallpaper.

3. Select the file you want to use and click the Open button.

4. If necessary, change how the image is displayed by opening the Display drop-down list and selecting Tile, Center, or Stretch. You see a preview of the image (this is my favorite tennis player, Patrick Rafter, at Wimbledon).

If you are viewing Web pages and see an image that you want to use as wallpaper, you can just right-click the image and choose Set as Wallpaper from the shortcut menu.

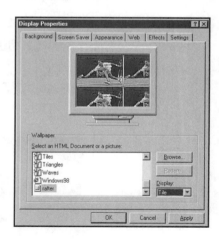

5. Click the OK button. The wallpaper is added to the desktop.

169

Editing the Pattern

If you don't like any of the patterns, create your own. You can edit the repeating pattern that is used by following these steps:

1. Right-click the desktop and select Properties from the shortcut menu that appears. The Display Properties dialog box appears, with the Background tab selected.

2. Click the Pattern button. You see the Pattern dialog box.

3. Click the pattern you want to start with. You start with an existing pattern and edit it. Select a pattern that is closest to what you want.

4. Click the Edit Pattern button. You see the Pattern Editor.

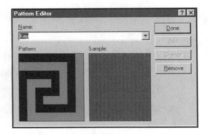

5. Type a name for this new pattern.

6. Edit the pattern. Click a box to change its color from green to black or vice versa. You see the pattern and how the desktop looks with the pattern as you edit.

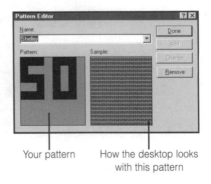

Your pattern   How the desktop looks
with this pattern

7. When you are finished making changes, click the Done button. Click the Yes button to save the pattern. When you return to the Pattern dialog box, your pattern is selected.

8. Click OK to close the Pattern dialog box.

9. Click OK to close the Display Properties dialog box.

Changing Individual Colors

If none of the predefined color schemes suit your fancy, design your own. You can select the color used for each onscreen item. You can also save the set of colors as your own personalized color scheme. Follow these steps:

1. Right-click the desktop and select Properties from the shortcut menu. The Display Properties dialog box appears.

2. Click the Appearance tab. You see the current scheme as well as how each element appears in this selected scheme.

3. Click the item you want to modify in the sample area. For instance, to change the color of the Active Window title bar, click it. You see the name of the item and the settings used for size, color, and font.

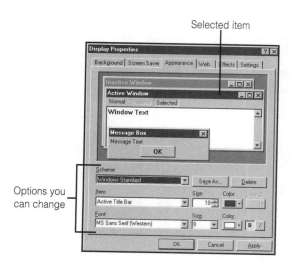

Selected item

Options you can change

4. Make any changes to the color, font, size, and other options. (These vary depending on what type of item you have selected.)

5. Follow steps 3 and 4 for each item you want to change.

6. To save your selected settings, click the Save As button. Type a name for the scheme and click OK.

7. Click OK to use the new scheme.

Cheat Sheet

Using a Screen Saver

1. Right-click the desktop and select Properties.
2. Click the Screen Saver tab.
3. Display the Screen Saver drop-down list and select the screen saver you want.
4. In the Wait text box, enter the number of minutes you want Windows to wait before displaying the image.
5. Click the OK button.

Stopping a Screen Saver

1. Move the mouse or press any key on the keyboard.

Using a Password

1. Right-click the desktop and select Properties.
2. Click the Screen Saver tab.
3. Display the Screen Saver drop-down list and select the screen saver you want.
4. In the Wait text box, enter the number of minutes you want Windows to wait before displaying the image.
5. Check the Password protected check box and then click the Change button.
6. Type the password twice, once in each text box.
7. Click the OK button.
8. When prompted that the password has been set, click the OK button.
9. Click OK.

30

Using a Screen Saver

If you left an image onscreen for a long time on older PC monitors, that image could become burned in. (You can sometimes see a burned-in image on ATM machines.) To prevent burn-in, someone came up with the idea of a screen saver. If you didn't use your computer for a certain period of time, the computer would automatically display an animated graphic, which would prevent burn-in.

Today's monitors don't have burn-in problems, but some users still use a screen saver, mostly for show. If you don't use your PC for a certain amount of time, Windows displays a moving graphic image. Windows includes several screen savers you can try.

Basic Survival

Using a Screen Saver

To see a preview, click the Preview button.

Follow these steps to use a screen saver:

1. Right-click the desktop and select Properties from the shortcut menu. The Display Properties dialog box appears.

2. Click the Screen Saver tab.

3. Display the Screen Saver drop-down list and select the screen saver you want.

Preview

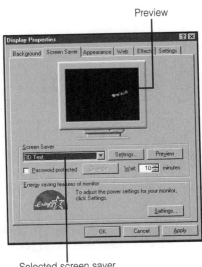

Selected screen saver

4. In the Wait text box, enter the number of minutes you want Windows to wait before displaying the image.

5. Click the OK button.

Windows displays the screen saver after the allotted wait time of inactivity has passed. To stop the screen saver and return to your program, press any key or move the mouse.

If you want to turn off the screen saver, follow these same steps, but select None from the Screen Saver drop-down list.

Beyond Survival

Using a Password

You can add a tiny bit of system security by assigning a password. Anyone that tries to deactivate the screen saver has to type the password. Keep in mind that you can always reboot the computer to get past the screen saver, so this security isn't all that secure.

To assign a password, follow these steps:

1. Right-click the desktop and select Properties from the shortcut menu. The Display Properties dialog box appears.

2. Click the Screen Saver tab.

3. Display the Screen Saver drop-down list and select the screen saver you want.

4. In the Wait text box, enter the number of minutes you want Windows to wait before displaying the image.

5. Check the Password protected check box and then click the Change button.

Type the password once in each text box.

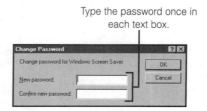

6. Type the password twice: once to set the password in the New password text box and once to confirm the password in the Confirm new password text box. Click the OK button. When prompted that the password has been set, click the OK button.

7. In the Display Properties dialog box, click the OK button to use the screen saver with the password.

When you set a password and want to deactivate the screen saver, Windows displays the Windows Screen Saver dialog box. Type your password and click the OK button.

Changing Screen Saver Options

You can modify how the screen saver appears. For instance, you can change the text used for the 3D Text screen saver or select a speed for some of the patterns. (Depending on the screen saver, the options vary.) Follow these steps:

1. Right-click the desktop and select Properties from the shortcut menu. The Display Properties dialog box appears.

2. Click the Screen Saver tab.

177

3. Display the Screen Saver drop-down list and select the screen saver you want.

4. In the Wait text box, enter the number of minutes you want Windows to wait before displaying the image.

5. Click the Settings button. Make any changes to the settings. The following figure shows the options you can select for 3D Text. Click the OK button.

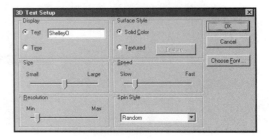

6. Click the OK button to close the Display Properties dialog box.

Cheat Sheet

Viewing Active Desktop

1. Right-click a blank area of the desktop and then select Properties.
2. Click the Web tab.
3. Check the View my Active Desktop as a Web page check box.
4. To display the Channel bar, check Internet Explorer Channel Bar.
5. Click the OK button.

Viewing Channels

1. In the Channel bar, click the category you want to view.
2. To see a preview, click the channel.
3. Click the Connect button and then follow your logon procedures to get connected to the Internet.
4. From the preview page, click the Add Active Channel button.
5. In the Modify Channel Usage dialog box, select how to handle the channel subscription.
6. Click the OK button.

31

Viewing Web Content on Your Desktop

If you have used the Internet, you may be comfortable with that method for viewing Web content. When you browse content, you can click a link to display the contents. You can set up your desktop to browse its contents just like a Web page. You also can display Web channels that you can use to browse the Internet. (For more on browsing the Internet, see Part 6, "Connecting to the Internet.")

Basic Survival

Viewing Active Desktop

The name of the feature used to browse Internet content from your desktop is called Active Desktop. You can turn this feature on and browse several channels. Keep in mind that to access content from the Internet, you must be connected. Or you can download the content for later viewing. Follow these steps:

You can also use the Folder Options to set up how folders are displayed. See Part 3, "File Basics," for information on working in Web view for folders.

1. Right-click a blank area of the desktop and then select Properties.

2. Click the Web tab.

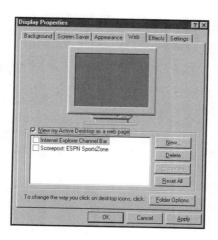

3. Check the View my Active Desktop as a Web page check box.

4. To display the Channel bar, check Internet Explorer Channel Bar.

5. Click the OK button.

The desktop is displayed with the Channel bar.

Use the Channel bar to view
content from the Internet.

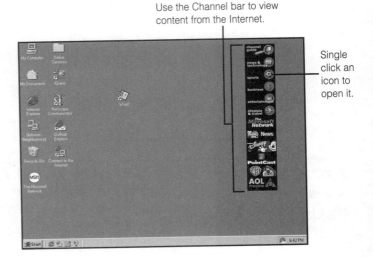

Single click an icon to open it.

To go back to the regular desktop, right-click a blank area of the desktop, choose Active Desktop, and uncheck View As Web Page by choosing this command.

Beyond Survival

Viewing Channels

Web channels are sites specifically designed for Internet Explorer. You can have content from any of these channels delivered right to your desktop. The Channel bar includes a channel guide, the channels you have set up (and some that are set up for you, such as MSNBC News), and several categories, each with different channels. To view the other available channels, follow these steps:

1. Click the category you want to view. Windows displays the available channels in the category (here, sports).

2. To see a preview, click the channel. You are prompted to connect to the Internet. (You can connect before you set up the desktop and click the channel, if you want.)

3. Click the Connect button and then follow your logon procedures to get connected to the Internet. You see the preview page for the selected channel.

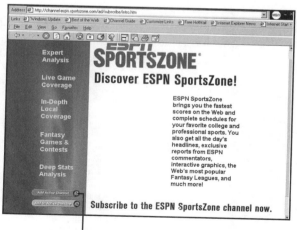

Click this button
to add a channel.

4. Click the Add Active Channel button to add the channel to the Channel bar and set up your subscription. You see the Modify Channel Usage dialog box. Here you can select how to handle the channel subscription (basically whether you are notified and when the content changes). There is no charge for subscribing to a channel.

You can also add the channel to the desktop. To do so, click the Add to Active Desktop button and then follow the steps for setting up the channel for the desktop.

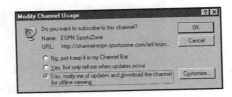

5. Select whether you just want the channel in the Channel bar, whether you want to subscribe and be notified when changes occur, or whether you want to subscribe, be notified, and automatically download content.

6. Click the OK button. The channel is added to your desktop.

To unsubscribe, open the Favorites menu in any Internet Explorer window. Then select Manage Subscriptions. You see the Subscriptions list. Right-click the channel you want to unsubscribe and select Delete. Confirm the deletion.

Cheat Sheet

Moving the Taskbar

1. Click a blank area of the taskbar and hold down the mouse button.
2. Drag the taskbar to another edge of the screen.

Resizing the Taskbar

1. Position the mouse pointer on the taskbar edge that borders the desktop.
2. Drag the border to the size you want.

Selecting Taskbar Options

1. Open the Start menu, select Settings, and select Taskbar.
2. Make any changes to the options.
3. Click OK.

32

Changing the Taskbar

The taskbar is within easy reach right at the bottom of your screen. If you don't want it displayed, or if you want to move it to a different location, you can do so. You can also change how the taskbar appears.

Basic Survival

Moving the Taskbar

To move the taskbar, follow these steps:

1. Click a blank area of the taskbar and hold down the mouse button.

2. Drag the taskbar to another edge of the screen.

When you release the mouse button, the taskbar appears in the new location.

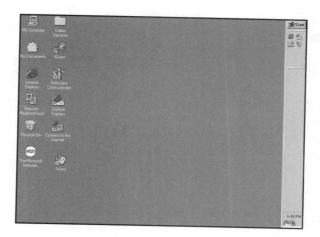

Resizing the Taskbar

To resize the taskbar, follow these steps:

1. Position the mouse pointer on the taskbar edge that borders the desktop. The pointer becomes a two-headed arrow.

2. Drag the border to the size you want.

The taskbar is resized.

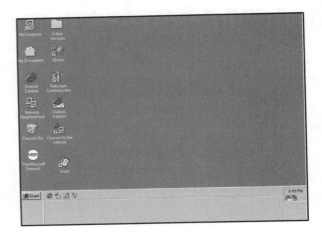

Beyond Survival

**Selecting
Taskbar
Options**

Follow these steps to set taskbar options:

1. Open the Start menu, select Settings, and select Taskbar. You see the Taskbar Properties dialog box.

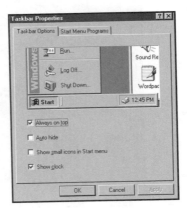

2. Make any changes to the following options:

Check the Always on top option to have the taskbar always appear on top of any other window on the screen.

Check the Auto hide option to have Windows hide the taskbar from view. You can make the taskbar pop up by moving the mouse pointer to the bottom edge of the screen.

Check Show small icons in the Start menu to use smaller icons for items in the Start menu.

Check Show clock to display the clock. Uncheck this option to turn off the clock.

3. Click the OK button.

Cheat Sheet

Installing a New Program

1. Insert the installation disk in the drive.
2. Click the Start button, select Settings, and then select Control Panel.
3. Double-click the Add/Remove Programs icon.
4. If necessary, click the Install/Uninstall tab.
5. Click the Install button.
6. When Windows finds the installation file on the disk, click the Finish button to run this program.
7. Follow the onscreen instructions for installing that particular program.

Uninstalling a Program

1. Click the Start button, select Settings, and then select Control Panel.
2. Double-click the Add/Remove Programs icon.
3. If necessary, click the Install/Uninstall tab.
4. Select the program you want to uninstall.
5. Click the Add/Remove button.

Adding Windows Components

1. Click the Start button, select Settings, and then select Control Panel.
2. Double-click the Add/Remove Programs icon.
3. Click the Windows Setup tab.
4. Check the components you want to install.
5. Click the OK button.
6. When prompted, insert the Windows disks or CD-ROM.

33

Installing and Uninstalling Programs

When you purchase a new PC, that system may come with some software programs. These programs might be enough to get you started, but as you use the PC more and more, you may find that you require other programs. (You can learn about the different program types in Chapter 4, "Software Defined.") You may want to upgrade an existing program to the newest version, or you may want to purchase an entirely new program. In this case, you need to install this new program.

And the reverse is also true. If you no longer use a program, you can uninstall it and free up some space on your hard disk.

Finally, when Windows is installed, some components may not have been set up. You can check and add other Windows components. Or if you want to save space, you can remove components.

Basic Survival

Purchasing a New Program

You can find software in some retail stores, in computer stores, and through mail order outlets. Scan through any computer magazine to get an idea of what programs are available as well as the cost. You can also use the Internet as a resource for researching and finding programs. You can even find freeware and shareware at many Internet sites. *Freeware programs* are provided free to you. *Shareware programs* are provided to you to try without cost. If you like the program, you can pay a small fee to register and continue using the program.

Scan a computer magazine's advertisements to see what software is available.

When you are looking for new programs to purchase, be sure that you can run that program on your system. Each program has system requirements—the type of microprocessor, amount of memory, hard disk space, video card, and any other required equipment. You can usually find these requirements printed on the side of the software box. Check the requirements to be sure your PC is capable of running the software.

Also, be sure that you get the right program for your system. If you have Windows 98, get Windows 98 programs. You can also purchase and run older DOS and Windows 3.1 programs on Windows 95 and Windows 98. If you have a Macintosh, get Macintosh programs. Most popular programs come in several versions.

As a final precaution, check to see how the software is distributed—on floppy disks or on a CD-ROM. If you have both a floppy disk and CD-ROM drive, you don't have to worry. But if you don't have a CD-ROM drive, be sure to get the version on floppy disks. CD-ROMs have become the most popular method for distributing programs, especially large programs.

Installing a New Program

When you install a new program, the installation program copies the necessary program files from the disk(s) to your hard disk and also sets up program icon(s) for the program. You need to specify which folder to use for the program files, where to place the program icons in the Start menu, and what program options you want to set. The options vary depending on the program, but you don't have to worry because the installation program guides you step-by-step through the process. You simply have to get the installation program started.

Windows provides an Add/Remove Programs icon that you can use to install new programs and remove (or uninstall programs). Follow these steps:

1. Click the Start button, select Settings, and then select Control Panel. You see the program icons in the Control Panel.

2. Double-click the Add/Remove Programs icon.

3. If necessary, click the Install/Uninstall tab. You see the options for installing and uninstalling programs.

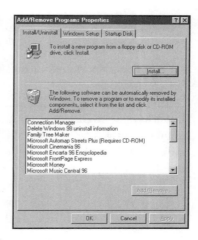

4. Click the Install button. You are prompted to insert the disk.

5. Insert the installation disk in the drive and click the Next button. If you are installing from a CD-ROM, that disc may have an AutoRun feature. If so, when you insert the disc, the installation program starts automatically.

Windows looks on the floppy drive and CD-ROM for an installation program. It then displays the name of this program in the dialog box. If this isn't the correct file, or if Windows can't find the file, you can type the path or use the Browse button to select the Installation program file.

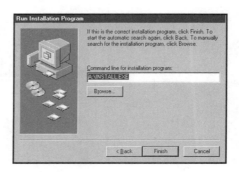

6. Click the Finish button to run this program. Windows starts the program's installation program.

7. Follow the onscreen instructions for installing that particular program.

Uninstalling a Program

If you have a program you no longer need, or if you upgrade a program and want to get rid of the previous version, you can uninstall it. You could simply delete the program folder, but keep in mind that the original program installation may have put files in other folders and also changed some system settings. The best way to uninstall the program is by using the Add/Remove Program icon. Follow these steps:

1. Click the Start button, select Settings, and then select Control Panel. You see the program icons in the Control Panel.

2. Double-click the Add/Remove Programs icon.

3. If necessary, click the Install/Uninstall tab. You see the options for installing and uninstalling programs.

4. Select the program you want to uninstall. If the program is not listed in this dialog box, you cannot use this method. Check the program documentation for information on uninstalling the program.

Selected program for removal ⎯⎯⎯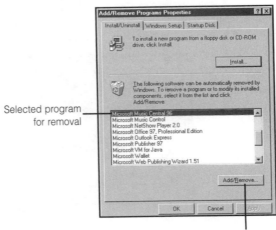

Click this button to remove.

5. Click the Add/Remove button. Windows removes the program files and any shortcuts to the program. You may be prompted to confirm the removal of certain files. If so, click OK or Yes to remove these files.

Beyond Survival

Using the Run Command to Install a Program

You can also install a program by using the Run command to run the installation program. To use this method, you need to know the exact name of the program. It's usually named something like INSTALL.EXE or SETUP.EXE. Follow these steps to use the Run command:

1. Insert the program disk into the drive.

2. Click the Start button.

3. Select the Run command. The Run dialog box appears.

4. In the Open text box, type the program name. Remember to type the drive letter. Your floppy drive is usually the A:drive. Your CD-ROM drive is usually the D:drive.

   If you aren't sure of the name of the installation program, type the drive name and then use the Browse button to browse through the files on that drive. Select the installation file.

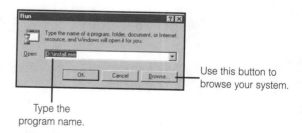

Type the
program name.

Use this button to
browse your system.

5. Click the OK button.

6. Follow the onscreen instructions for installing the program.

Adding Windows Components

When you install Windows, you have some options on which program components are installed. If you did not install Windows yourself—or if you just want to add other components (games, wallpaper, other program features)—you can do so using the Add/Remove Programs icon. Follow these steps:

1. Click the Start button, select Settings, and select Control Panel. You see the program icons in the Control Panel.

2. Double-click the Add/Remove Programs icon.

3. Click the Windows Setup tab. You see the Windows components. Items in the Components list that are checked are installed. Items that are blank are not installed. If there's a gray background and a check, only some of the items in that set are installed.

4. Check the components you want to install. Some components, such as Accessories, include more than one component. To view the available options, select the component and then click the Details button. Check which components you want to install and then click the OK button.

5. Click the OK button.

6. When prompted, insert the Windows disks or CD-ROM. The necessary program files are copied to your Windows folder, and this component is added.

Cheat Sheet

Changing the Date and Time

1. Right-click the time in the taskbar and select Adjust Date/Time.
2. Make any changes to the date. You can display the Month drop-down list to select a different month and then click the appropriate date on the calendar. Use the year spin box to increment the year.
3. Make any changes to the time. You can click the time in the clock or use the spin boxes to increment the hour, minutes, or seconds.
4. Click the OK button.

Changing the Time Zone

1. Right-click the time in the taskbar and select Adjust Date/Time.
2. Click the Time Zone tab.
3. Display the drop-down list and select the appropriate time zone.
4. Check whether you want to adjust for daylight savings.
5. Click the OK button.

Changing Regional Settings

1. Click Start, select Settings, and select Control Panel.
2. Double-click the Regional Settings icon.
3. Display the drop-down list on the Regional Settings tab and select the country.
4. Review (and make changes to if necessary) each of the other dialog box tabs and their options.
5. Click the OK button.

34

Changing the System Date and Time

Windows uses the system date and time to stamp files. This way you can keep track of when a file was created, modified, accessed, and so on. The current time is also displayed in the taskbar for your convenience. If the date and time are wrong, you can easily change them.

If you use your computer in another country, you may also want to change the regional settings. These changes affect how dates, times, currency, and numbers are displayed.

Basic Survival

Changing the Date and Time

To change the date and time, follow these steps:

1. Right-click the time in the taskbar and select Adjust Date/Time. You see the Date/Time Properties dialog box.

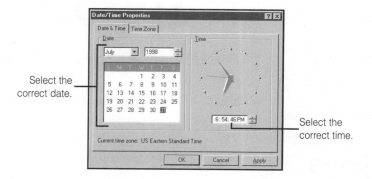

Select the correct date.

Select the correct time.

Shortcut: Double-click the time to open the Date/Time dialog box.

2. Make any changes to the date. You can display the Month drop-down list to select a different month and click the appropriate date on the calendar. Use the year spin box to increment the year.

3. Make any changes to the time. You can click the time in the clock or use the spin boxes to increment the hour, minutes, or seconds.

4. Click the OK button.

Beyond Survival

Changing the Time Zone

You can also use the Date/Time Properties dialog box to select a time zone. And you can select whether the clock is automatically adjusted for daylight savings time. Follow these steps:

1. Right-click the time in the taskbar and select Adjust Date/Time. You see the Date/Time Properties dialog box.

2. Click the Time Zone tab.

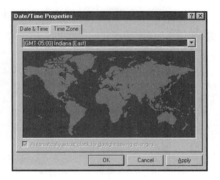

3. Display the drop-down list and select the appropriate time zone.

4. Check whether you want to adjust for daylight savings.

5. Click the OK button.

Changing Regional Settings

If you are used to a different format for displaying dates, times, or numbers, you may want to select a different regional setting. You can select from several countries and also change each format for individual items (number, currency, date, and time). Follow these steps to make a change:

1. Click Start, select Settings, and select Control Panel. You see the programs in the Control Panel.

2. Double-click the Regional Settings icon. You see the Regional Settings Properties dialog box.

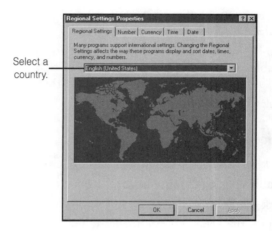

Select a country.

3. To change to a different country, display the drop-down list on the Regional Settings tab and select the country.

4. Review (and make changes to if necessary) each of the other dialog box tabs and their options.

5. Click the OK button.

Cheat Sheet

Switching Mouse Buttons

1. Click Start, select Settings, and select Control Panel.
2. Double-click the Mouse icon.
3. In the Button configuration section, select Right-handed or Left-handed.
4. If you have trouble double-clicking, adjust the speed by dragging the Double-click speed slider left (slower) or right (faster). You can test the speed by double-clicking the jack-in-the-box image.
5. Click the OK button.

Using Different Pointers

1. Click Start, select Settings, and select Control Panel.
2. Double-click the Mouse icon.
3. Click the Pointers tab.
4. Display the Scheme drop-down list and select the scheme you want to use.
5. Click the OK button.

Changing the Pointer Speed and Adding a Pointer Trail

1. Click Start, select Settings, and select Control Panel.
2. Double-click the Mouse icon.
3. Click the Motion tab.
4. Make your changes and click the OK button.

35

Changing How the Mouse Works

If needed, you can make adjustments to how the mouse works. One change is especially useful if you are left-handed. You can switch the mouse buttons so that you can click the right mouse button for left-clicking and vice versa. You can also adjust the double-click speed, use pointers, and make other changes.

Note that if you have a Microsoft IntelliMouse, you see different options. You can select any of the available options for this type of mouse.

Basic Survival

Switching Buttons

The most common mouse change is to switch the left and right buttons. Follow these steps to make a change:

1. Click Start, select Settings, and select Control Panel. You see the programs in the Control Panel.

2. Double-click the Mouse icon. You see the Mouse Properties dialog box.

Select mouse buttons here.

Adjust double-click speed here.

Test double-click speed here.

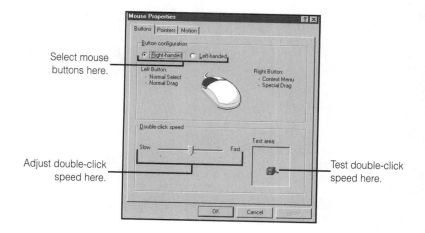

3. In the Button configuration section, select Right-handed or Left-handed. (If you are using a Microsoft IntelliMouse, this option appears on the Basics tab.)

4. If you have trouble double-clicking, adjust the speed by dragging the Double-click speed slider left (slower) or right (faster). You can test the speed by double-clicking the jack-in-the-box image.

5. Click the OK button.

Beyond Survival

Using Different Pointers

Another change you can make to the mouse is to select different pointers. For most key actions, the mouse pointer changes its shape to indicate what it is doing. You see one shape, for instance, when the system is busy. You see another shape when you are selecting text. You can select a different set of pointers (called a scheme) by following these steps:

1. Click Start, select Settings, and select Control Panel. You see the programs in the Control Panel.

2. Double-click the Mouse icon. You see the Mouse Properties dialog box.

3. Click the Pointers tab. You see the default set of pointers.

4. Display the Scheme drop-down list and select the scheme you want to use. You see a preview of each pointer type in the new scheme.

5. Click the OK button.

Changing the Pointer Speed and Adding a Pointer Trail

As another possibility, you can change the pointer speed and add a trail to the pointer. Adding a trail helps you see the path of the mouse. Follow these steps:

1. Click Start, select Settings, and select Control Panel. You see the programs in the Control Panel.

2. Double-click the Mouse icon. You see the Mouse Properties dialog box.

3. Click the Motion tab.

4. Drag the Pointer speed slider left or right to make it move slower or faster. (If you are using a Microsoft IntelliMouse, this option appears on the Basics tab.)

5. To show a trail for the pointer, check the Show pointer trails and then drag the slider bar to select a length. (If you are using a Microsoft IntelliMouse, this option appears on the Visibility tab.)

6. Click the OK button.

Cheat Sheet

Adding Sounds to Events

1. Open the Start menu, select Settings, and select Control Panel.
2. Double-click the Sounds icon.
3. To play a sound associated with an event, click the event and click the Play button.
4. To attach a sound to an event or to change the sound currently attached to an event, click the event in the Events list. Then select a sound file from the Name list.
5. Click the OK button when you're finished.

Playing Music

1. Click the Start button, select Programs, select Accessories, select Entertainment, and select CD Player.
2. Insert a disc into your CD drive and click the Play button.

Playing Sounds

1. Click the Start button, select Programs, select Accessories, select Entertainment, and select Sound Recorder.
2. Open the File menu and select Open. Change to the drive and folder that contains the sound file.
3. When you see the sound file you want to play, double-click it. To play the sound, click the Play button.

Playing Media Clips and Movies

1. Click the Start button, select Programs, select Accessories, select Entertainment, and select Media Player.
2. Open the File menu and select Open. Change to the drive and folder that contains the media file.
3. When you see the file you want to play, double-click it. Click the Play button.

36

Playing Sounds and Music

You may have noticed that when you make a mistake or click somewhere you shouldn't, you sometimes hear a sound. You may also hear sounds for other events. That's because you can have Windows play a sound when a certain event happens. You can select which events sounds are played for and which sound is played.

You also have other multimedia features you can use with Windows. You can play an audio CD, play sound files, and even record sounds. You can also play multimedia files.

Multimedia is the combination of different media—sound, video, text, graphics, animation, and so on. For example, you might have a multimedia encyclopedia. When you look up an entry for Beethoven, you can not only read a text account of his life and accomplishments, but also play a sample of one of his symphonies. The entry might also include a picture of the famous composer.

To take advantage of these multimedia programs, you need a CD-ROM drive, sound card, and speakers. As multimedia presentations and programs became more popular, the equipment to run these features became standard equipment on a PC. If you have a new PC, you probably have a PC with this equipment. If you don't, you can purchase a multimedia upgrade package to add this equipment.

Basic Survival

Adding Sounds to Events

You can review the associated sounds Windows plays and make any changes by following these steps:

1. Open the Start menu, select Settings, and select Control Panel.

2. Double-click the Sounds icon. You see the Sounds Properties dialog box. Events that already have sounds attached to them are marked with a speaker icon.

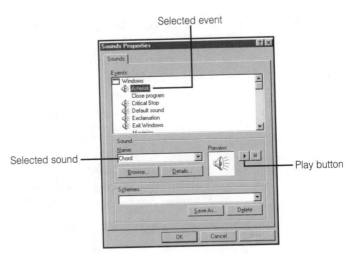

Selected event

Selected sound ——

Play button

3. To play a sound associated with an event, click the event and click the Play button.

4. To attach a sound to an event or to change the sound currently attached to an event, click the event in the Events list. Then select a sound file from the Name list.

5. Click the OK button when you're finished.

Playing Music

If you like music, you can use the CD Player application (included with Windows 95 and Windows 98) to play your audio CDs. Keep in mind that the sound quality isn't going to be as great as if you were playing the CDs on your CD player. Even though most sound cards come with speakers that are adequate for playing sounds, don't expect excellent quality.

To play a CD, follow these steps:

1. Click the Start button, select Programs, select Accessories, select Multimedia (Windows 95) or Entertainment (Windows 98), and (finally) select CD Player. Windows starts the CD Player program.

Stop button

2. Insert a disc into your CD drive and click the Play button. CD Player plays the first track on the CD. You can see the current track number and amount of time the CD has been playing in the CD Player window.

You can minimize the CD Player window, and the CD continues to play. Some systems have an AutoRun command that automatically starts the CD when you insert it into the drive.

Playing Sounds

Not only can you play audio CDs on your computer, you also can play other sounds. For instance, a coworker may have recorded a message and attached it to a file. You can play the sound.

Sounds, like all information on a computer, are stored in files. Most sound files are WAV files. You can play back sounds that you have recorded or sounds provided with some other application. You also can download sounds from bulletin board systems or the Internet. And you can purchase sound files.

To play a sound, follow these steps:

1. Click the Start button, select Programs, select Accessories, select Multimedia (Windows 95) or Entertainment (Windows 98), and select Sound Recorder. Windows displays the Sound Recorder window.

2. Open the File menu and select Open. In the Open dialog box that appears, change to the drive and folder that contains the file. Windows includes some sample sound files in the WINDOWS\MEDIA folder.

3. When you see the sound file you want to play, double-click it. In the Sound Recorder window, the name of the sound appears in the title bar.

209

4. To play the sound, click the Play button. Sound Recorder plays the sound. As it plays, you see the sound wave in the Sound Recorder window.

Beyond Survival

Playing a Different Track on a CD

You can select which track is played on the CD and also use the toolbar to control play. You can also enter the name of the artist, CD, and tracks.

To enter the name of the artist, CD, and tracks, follow these steps:

1. Insert the audio CD in the CD-ROM drive. In the CD Player window, open the Disc menu and select the Edit Play List command. You see the CD Player: Disc Settings dialog box.

Type the artist name. Type the title here.

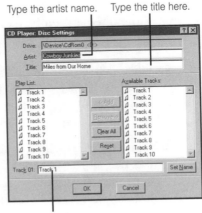

Type the track name.

2. Type the name in the Artist text box.

3. Type the name of the CD in the Title text box.

4. To enter a track name, select the track in the Play List, type the name, and click Set Name.

5. When you are done making changes, click the OK button.

To play a different track, follow these steps:

1. In the CD Player window, display the Track drop-down list.

2. Click the track you want to play.

The CD Player includes buttons that enable you to start a song over, switch to a different song, stop a song, and so on. Point to a button and pause to display the button's name. These buttons are described in the following table.

Name	Description
Play	Starts playing the CD.
Pause	Pauses the CD. To resume play, click the Play button again.
Stop	Stops the CD.
Previous Track	Plays the previous track.
Next Track	Plays the next track.
Skip Forward	Moves forward within the current track.
Skip Backward	Moves backward within the current track.
Eject	Ejects the CD.

Recording Sounds

To record sounds, you need a sound card and a microphone, and the microphone must be plugged into your sound card. Most sound cards come with a microphone, but it may not have been connected. Check your sound card manual for help on where to plug in the microphone.

Follow these steps to record a sound:

1. In the Sound Recorder window, open the File menu and select New.

2. Click the Record button to start recording.

3. Speak into the microphone to record your sound. You see a visual representation of the sound wave as you make your recording. Because sound files can be really huge, you should try to keep your message short and concise.

4. When you finish recording, click the Stop button. You can play back the sound by clicking the Play button.

5. To save the sound, open the File menu and select Save. The Save As dialog box appears.

6. In the Save As dialog box, change to the drive and folder where you want to store the file. Then type a filename in the File name text box and click the Save button.

Playing Media Clips and Movies

If you have multimedia presentations, you can use the Windows Media Player to play them back. (Windows includes some sample files in the WINDOWS\MEDIA folder.) You can play back the following types of files:

- Video for Windows (AVI files)
- Sound (WAV files)
- MIDI music files (MID and RMI)

Many Internet sites also include movies that you can play back.

Follow these steps to play a media file:

1. Click the Start button, select Programs, select Accessories, select Multimedia (Windows 95) or Entertainment (Windows 98), and select Media Player. Windows displays the Media Player program.

2. Open the File menu and select Open. The Open dialog box appears with the Media folder selected. You can open files in this folder. Or if necessary, change to the appropriate drive and folder.

3. When you see the file you want to play, double-click it. You see the Media Player window with the name of the file in the title bar.

4. To play the clip, click the Play button. Media Player plays back the media clip.

Cheat Sheet

Installing a New Printer

1. Click the Start button, select Settings, and select Printers.
2. Double-click the Add Printer icon.
3. Click the Next button to continue with the installation.
4. Select the Manufacturers name from the list. Then select the printer's name. Click Next.
5. Select the appropriate port and click Next.
6. Enter a name for the printer, or accept the one Windows has given it.
7. Select whether you want the new printer to be the default printer. Then click the Next button.
8. Select whether you want to print a test page. If so, Windows prints a test page, and you are asked whether it printed successfully. Click Yes.
9. Click the Finish button.

Handling Print Jobs

1. Click the Start button, select Settings, and then select Printers.
2. Double-click the printer you want to view.
3. To pause a print job, open the Printer menu and select Pause Printing. To restart, open the Printer menu and uncheck Pause Printing.
4. To cancel a print job, select the job you want to cancel. Open the Document menu and select Cancel Printing.
5. To close the printer window, click its Close (X) button.

37

Setting Up a Printer

If you purchase a new printer or add a printer, you need to set it up. Windows includes a wizard that leads you step by step through the process. You can also use the Printer Control Panel to change printer options.

When you are printing, you may need a way to view and change the jobs being printed. The print queue lists the documents that you have sent to a printer, and it shows how far along the printing is. Using the print queue, you can pause, restart, or cancel print jobs.

Basic Survival

Installing a New Printer

You can add a new printer to your Windows setup using a step-by-step guide called a *wizard*. Use the wizard anytime you get a new printer or change printers.

For more information on setting up and using a network printer, see Part 7, "Networking."

Follow these steps to set up a new printer:

1. Click the Start button, select Settings, and select Printers. You see the Printers folder.

2. Double-click the Add Printer icon. The Add Printer Wizard dialog box appears.

3. Click the Next button to continue with the installation.

Select the manufacturer here.

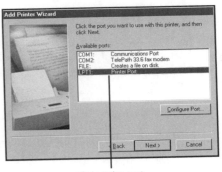

Select the printer here.

4. Select a name from the Manufacturers list. Select the name of the Printer and click Next.

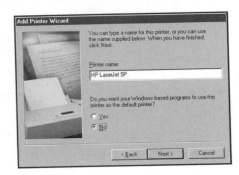

Select the port.

5. Select the appropriate port and click Next.

6. Enter a name for the printer, or accept the one Windows has given it.

7. Select whether you want the new printer to be the default printer. Then click the Next button.

Click the Back button if you need to go back a step.

8. Select whether you want to print a test page. If so, Windows prints a test page, and you are asked whether it printed successfully. Click Yes.

9. Click the Finish button. Windows then adds the new printer's icon to the Printers folder.

Handling Print Jobs

While the printer is printing, you see the printer icon in the taskbar. If needed, you can view the print queue to see which jobs are printing and to check the status of a print job. For short documents, you may not have time to see the queue; the data is sent to the printer and processed too quickly. For longer jobs or multiple jobs, you can view the print queue and make changes, if needed.

For instance, you may want to pause printing when you have a change to make in the text or when you want to load a different paper type, for example. If you discover an error in the job you are printing or if you decide you need to add something before printing the job, you can cancel the print job.

Follow these steps to display the print queue:

1. Click the Start button, select Settings, and select Printers. You see the Printers folder.

Shortcut: Double-click the printer icon in the taskbar to display the print queue.

2. Double-click the printer you want to view. The printer window displays a list of the documents in the queue plus statistics about the documents being printed. If the print queue window is empty, there is nothing in the print queue.

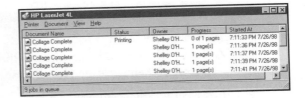

3. To pause a print job, open the Printer menu and select Pause Printing. To restart, open the Printer menu and uncheck Pause Printing.

4. To cancel a print job, select the job you want to cancel. Open the Document menu and select Cancel Printing.

5. To close the printer window, click its Close (X) button.

Beyond Survival

Setting the Default Printer

If you have more than one printer connected, you must select one as the default. The default printer is the printer your applications automatically use when you choose to print. Follow these steps to select a default printer:

1. Click the Start button, select Settings, and select Printers. You see the Printers folder.

2. Select the printer you want to choose as the default.

3. Open the File menu and select Set as Default.

You can always switch to another printer within an application. For instance, if you want to print an individual document to a different printer, you can select that printer. Choose the Print command for that program (usually File, Print), and then look for a printer drop-down list in the Print dialog box. Select the printer you want and then print your document.

PART 5

PC Maintenance

Just like your house or your car, your PC also requires some regular maintenance to achieve optimal performance. As you will soon see, most of the maintenance on your PC centers around your hard disk drive and your files and making sure that both remain healthy and viable. The following topics should help you keep your PC in top shape:

- Correcting Hard Disk Errors
- Scanning for Viruses
- Defragmenting Your Hard Disk
- Creating a Startup Disk
- Backing Up Your System
- Restoring Your Data from a Backup
- Installing New Hardware
- Troubleshooting Problems

Cheat Sheet

Using ScanDisk to Check for Errors in Windows 95 or 98

1. From the Start menu select Run.
2. In the Run dialog box, type **SCANDISK** and click OK.
3. Select the drive you want to scan.
4. Select a Standard or Thorough scan.
5. Select any advanced options for your scan and click OK.
6. Click the Start button in the dialog box to begin scanning.

Checking for Errors by Using CHKDSK

1. Exit any running programs.
2. Type **CHKDSK *X:* /F**, where *X:* is the drive you want to check, and press Enter.

   If lost clusters are found, CHKDSK saves them in files named file0001.chk, file0002.chk, and so on.
3. Delete any files created by CHKDSK.

Running Disk Cleanup

1. From the Start menu select Programs, Accessories, System Tools, and Disk Cleanup.
2. In the Disk Cleanup dialog box, select the type of files you want Disk Cleanup to scan for and remove.
3. Click OK to begin.

38

Correcting Hard Disk Errors

Maintenance on your hard disk is nothing like maintenance on your car—there is no chassis to lube, spark plugs to replace, or oil to change. In fact, there are no moving parts on your hard disk that you ever need to worry about. But, that doesn't mean that you should ignore routine hard disk maintenance.

Hard disk maintenance refers to how your hard disk drive stores files and steps you need to take to make sure that file storage is done in an efficient manner.

Normally, your hard disk is fairly efficient in the manner in which it stores your files. However, as you learned in Chapter 23, "Deleting and Undeleting Files," when you delete a file, the file is not actually removed from your hard disk drive. Instead, the file is moved to the Recycle Bin. The Recycle Bin is a special folder that holds files to be deleted. When a file is deleted from the Recycle Bin, the file's attributes are changed, indicating that the space used by the file you are deleting is now available (it is now considered "free space") and can be used by other files.

Occasionally, when a new file is created from this supply of "free space," not all the free space is used by the new file, and the result is a "lost cluster" or "lost chain." A lost cluster (or lost chain) is a portion of a previously deleted file that still appears as if it is being used by that file. It is essentially free space that isn't totally free and results in a loss of free space on your hard disk drive.

Basic Survival

Using ScanDisk to Check for Errors in Windows 95 or 98

If you are running either Windows 95 or Windows 98, you can use a utility program called ScanDisk to check your hard disk drive for errors. The ScanDisk utility you find in Windows 95 or Windows 98 is similar to its DOS counterpart, but it is a much more advanced utility.

To run ScanDisk in either Windows 95 or Windows 98:

1. From the Start menu, select Run to open the Run dialog box.

2. Type SCANDISK and click OK. (You can also access ScanDisk from the Start menu by selecting Programs, Accessories, System Tools, and ScanDisk.)

3. The Windows 95/98 version of ScanDisk allows you to not only select the drive you want to check, but also select to perform a Standard check that checks your files and folders for lost clusters, or you can select a Thorough check and also perform a surface scan of your hard disk drive. Select the drive you want to scan, and then select a Standard or Thorough scan.

4. ScanDisk also has a set of Advanced options that allow you even greater control in using the program. To access these options, click the Advanced button, select any advanced options for your scan, and click OK.

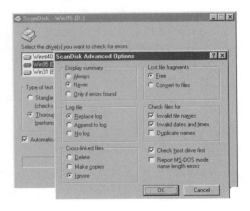

5. Click the Start button in the dialog box to begin scanning.

Beyond Survival

Using CHKDSK to Check Your Hard Disks

In early versions of MS-DOS (such as Version 6.0 and earlier), you received a handy utility program called CHKDSK (CHecK DiSK) that you could run periodically to check your hard disk drive for lost clusters and remove them.

Following are the steps you would take to use CHKDSK to check for and remove lost clusters on your hard disk drive:

1. Exit any programs you are running, including Windows.

2. Type CHKDSK X: /F, where *X:* is the drive you want to check such as C:, and press Enter. If you get an error message that says Bad command or filename, it means that DOS cannot find the CHKDSK program file. Type **\DOS\CHKDSK *X:* /F** and press Enter. CHKDSK begins checking the drive you designated and within a few seconds CHKDSK reports its findings.

Information supplied by CHKDSK

```
C:\DOS>chkdsk e:

Volume WIN31        created 08-03-1997 9:22p
Volume Serial Number is 415A-1EE6

1,049,329,664 bytes total disk space
      294,912 bytes in 7 hidden files
    1,900,544 bytes in 116 directories
  733,151,232 bytes in 3,814 user files
  313,982,976 bytes available on disk

       16,384 bytes in each allocation unit
       64,046 total allocation units on disk
       19,164 available allocation units on disk

      654,336 total bytes memory
      485,904 bytes free

Instead of using CHKDSK, try using SCANDISK.  SCANDISK can reliably detect
and fix a much wider range of disk problems.  For more information,
type HELP SCANDISK from the command prompt.

C:\DOS>
```

3. If CHKDSK finds any lost clusters, it asks you whether you want to save the lost clusters to a file. Answer Y and CHKDSK saves the lost clusters in files in the root directory of the drive you are checking. The files are named file0000.chk, file0001.chk, file0002.chk, and so on. You can safely delete any files in this format that you find on your PC.

Running ScanDisk from DOS

In versions of MS-DOS beginning with 6.2, CHKDSK was supplemented with another disk-checking program called ScanDisk. ScanDisk performs a more extensive check than CHKDSK, but can still be used to check for and remove lost clusters.

To run ScanDisk from DOS:

Don't use CHKDSK on a network drive if you are connected to a network.

1. Exit any programs you are running, including Windows.

2. Type **SCANDISK X:**, where *X:* is the drive you want to check such as C:, and press Enter. If you get an error message that says Bad command or filename, it means that DOS cannot find the ScanDisk program file. Type **\DOS\SCANDISK** X: and press Enter.

3. If ScanDisk uncovers any errors, it displays an error message and prompts you to either save the lost clusters in a file or delete the lost clusters.

   ScanDisk also gives you the option of creating an undo disk in case you want to undo what ScanDisk does.

   ScanDisk also checks your hard disk for physical problems by performing a scan of the physical surface of the disk.

You should perform a surface scan every few months.

4. After you finish scanning with ScanDisk, select Exit to return to the DOS prompt.

Finishing Up Where ScanDisk Leaves Off

After you use ScanDisk a few times, you might also want to try using a new utility that Microsoft has added to Windows 98—Disk Cleanup. Disk Cleanup scans your hard disk for files that are literally doing nothing more than taking up space.

To run Disk Cleanup, use the following steps:

1. From the Start menu, select Programs, Accessories, System Tools, and Disk Cleanup.

2. In the Disk Cleanup dialog box, select the type of files you want Disk Cleanup to scan for and remove. You can safely check all four categories of files to allow Disk Cleanup to perform a thorough cleanup job.

Select the type of files you want to remove.

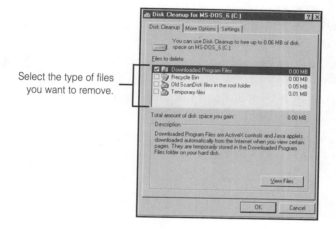

3. Click OK to begin.

225

Cheat Sheet

Common Sense Tips for Protecting Your PC from Viruses

- Install an antivirus program and make sure you regularly update the virus definition files.
- Scan all disks before you copy any files from them onto your PC.
- Write protect all program disks before installing the program to prevent possible infections. If you have a choice, purchase programs on CDs rather than disks because CDs cannot be "accidentally" infected.
- Never start or boot your PC with a disk in the drive.

Scanning for Viruses by Using Norton AntiVirus

1. Exit all programs you have running.
2. Open the Start menu and select Programs, Norton AntiVirus, and select the Norton AntiVirus icon to start the program.
3. Select the drive you want to scan by selecting the corresponding check box.
4. Click the Scan Now button to begin your scan.

39

Scanning for Viruses

Just as viral infections can severely debilitate you, computer viruses can wreak havoc with your PC. Computer viruses, although not biological in nature, can nonetheless be just as destructive as their biological namesakes. Computer viruses can run the gamut from being mildly annoying to being able to totally wipe out your programs and data.

Computer viruses are small programs that are so named because they mimic the behavior of actual viruses—they infect the host computer, spread from computer to computer, and eventually do something destructive.

The most common method of transmittal is by using a floppy disk infected with a virus, but your computer can also get infected from files you download from bulletin board services (BBSs) and from the Internet, as well as files attached to email messages you receive.

Basic Survival

Common Sense Tips for Protecting Your PC from Viruses

To protect your PC from computer viruses, you need to purchase an antivirus program and use it to scan your PC's hard disk drive. If your PC is infected with a virus, you can use the antivirus program to remove the virus.

But your first priority should be prevention. Following are a few suggestions for avoiding viruses:

- Make sure you have an antivirus program installed and running on your PC.

- Regularly (preferably every month or two) update the virus definitions in your antivirus program.

- Scan every floppy disk and email you receive before using or reading them.

• Never turn on or start your PC with a floppy disk in drive A: that you have never scanned.

Scanning Your PC with an Antivirus Program

There are several companies that produce PC antivirus programs. Two of the best known are Symantec (www.symantec.com), which produces Norton AntiVirus and McAfee (www.mcafee.com), which produces VirusScan. Both do an exceptional job of scanning your PC for viruses and removing any viruses that might be found, and both provide monthly virus definition updates to help you fight new viruses as they are produced.

If you select Norton AntiVirus from Symantec, following is what you need to do to install and use the program to scan your PC for viruses:

1. From the Start menu select Run and type **X:\SETUP.EXE** (where *X:* is the drive designation of your CD-ROM drive) from the CD-ROM program disk.

2. Accept all the default values presented during the program's installation.

3. When the installation is completed, from the Start menu select Programs, Norton AntiVirus, and select the Norton AntiVirus icon to start the program.

Click to begin scanning.

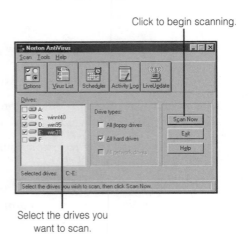

Select the drives you want to scan.

4. Make sure all drives you want to scan are checked in the Drives list on the left side of the window.

5. Click the Scan Now button to begin scanning the designated drives.

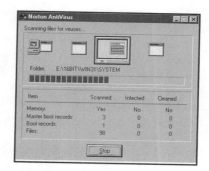

6. If the program detects a virus infecting your drive, it presents a warning message and several options for eradicating the virus.

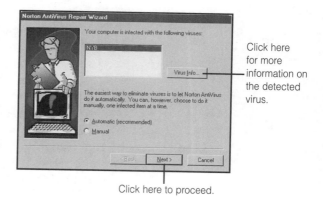

Click here for more information on the detected virus.

Click here to proceed.

Just as you can manually scan your PC's hard disk drives, you can also manually scan any floppy disks you acquire by simply selecting drive A: instead of your hard disk drives.

Regardless of which antivirus program you install, you should regularly scan your PC for viruses and most importantly, make sure you also regularly update your antiviral definition files by downloading the update files from the program's manufacturer.

229

Beyond Survival

Additional Virus-Checking Features

Every antivirus program on the market allows you to manually scan your disks for viruses. The best ones, however, allow you to load a program that automatically checks your disks and files without any intervention on your part.

Some programs refer to this feature as *auto-scan*. In Norton AntiVirus, it is called Auto-Protect. Make sure that whichever antivirus program you purchase and install allows you to set an auto-scan feature to protect your system from any files and (floppy) disks you encounter. The following figure displays the Auto-Protect options available in Norton AntiVirus.

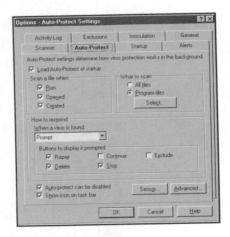

In addition to an auto-scan feature, most good antivirus programs also allow you to schedule a weekly scan of your entire system. The following figure shows the Program Scheduler window in Norton AntiVirus.

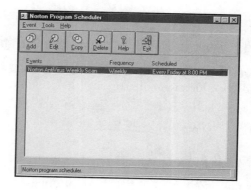

Another useful feature you find in Norton AntiVirus is the ability to work with your Web browser to automatically scan any
files you download from the Internet before you save them to
your hard disk. If you have Netscape already installed on your
PC, when you install Norton AntiVirus it prompts you to
install the program to automatically scan all files you download
using Netscape.

Cheat Sheet

Using the Windows 95/98 Disk Defragmenter Utility

1. From the Start menu, select Programs, Accessories, System Tools, and Disk Defragmenter to start the program.
2. If you have more than one drive in your PC, select the drive you want to defragment and click OK.

Using Nuts & Bolts' Disk Tune

1. Exit all programs you may have running.
2. From the Start menu, select Programs, Nuts & Bolts, and Disk Tune to start the disk defragmenter.
3. Select the drive you want to defragment and select the corresponding check box.
4. Click Next to begin the scan.
5. Repeat steps 3 and 4 for each hard disk drive in your PC.
6. Scan your hard disk drives on a regular basis, at least once a month, to maintain hard disk drive performance.

40

Defragmenting Your Hard Disk

Defragmentation is not a term that most people are totally familiar with, but one you should learn about so that you can determine how it fits into your PC maintenance plans. Before I can explain defragmentation, we need to review how files are stored on your hard disk.

Your PC's hard disk drives are divided into hundreds of concentric rings and each ring is further divided into storage sections called clusters. Cluster size varies according to which operating system (Windows 95/98, Windows NT, and so on) you are running, but the basic idea is the same. When you store a file on your disk drive, the operating system looks for the first empty, or available, cluster it can find to store the file. If the entire file won't fit into one cluster, the operating system places the next portion of the file into the next available cluster it finds—even if the clusters are not adjacent. This process is repeated with as many clusters as are needed to store the file.

The operating system keeps track of which files are scattered across your disk drive, and can easily reassemble files regardless of the number of clusters used to store the files. When you delete files, the operating system makes available the clusters that the file was stored in. After several weeks or months of creating and deleting files and having them scattered all over your hard disk drive, your files become fragmented. The operating system doesn't have a problem retrieving files that are scattered all over your hard disk drive. But, because the files are not in adjacent clusters, it takes longer to locate all the parts of a file whenever you run a program or open a file to work on, such as a word processing document or a spreadsheet.

Here's another example. When you go to the supermarket, all the grocery items you want to purchase are not always sitting on one shelf next to one another. You may have to go to aisle 1 to get milk and eggs. You may have to go to aisle 11 to get cereal, aisle 8 to get coffee, aisle 16 to get paper towels, and aisle 3 to get soda. Having the grocery items stored in different locations in the supermarket doesn't cause you any problems in doing your shopping; it just takes longer to find the items you want to purchase because you're hopping from aisle to aisle to retrieve them.

Of course, you can't rearrange the supermarket to make your shopping go more quickly. However, you can rearrange the files on your PC's hard disk so that it takes your operating system less time to find them. Rearranging your files or their scattered parts is called *defragmentation*.

Defragmenting your files is not essential. You can actually go for years without ever defragmenting your files, but the longer you put it off, the more fragmented your files become and the more time your operating system has to spend reassembling your fragmented files. Think of defragmentation as a routine efficiency chore.

Basic Survival

Using the Windows 95/98 Disk Defragmenter

Both Windows 95 and Windows 98 ship with a basic disk defragmenter utility. Although the program is a scaled-down version of the more elaborate version sold by Symantec, it is still quite capable of getting the job done for you.

To start defragmenting your hard drive:

1. From the Start menu select Programs, Accessories, System Tools, and Disk Defragmenter.

2. If you have more than one drive in your PC, select the drive you want to defragment, and click OK. Now just sit back and watch as the utility defragments the drive you selected, as shown here.

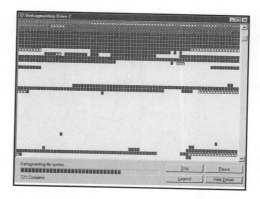

Defragment your hard disk on a regular basis.

You should try to defragment your hard drive at least once a week to start. If you find that the disk is not very fragmented, you might want to space the sessions out to once every two weeks.

Beyond Survival

Heavy Duty Disk Defragmenting

There are several good commercial defragmentation programs on the market, which run under Windows 95/98. Most come bundled with a suite of useful utilities that you can use for other maintenance operations. Two of the most popular are Speed Disk, which is part of the Norton Utilities, and Disk Tune, which is part of Nuts & Bolts. The following two figures show the defragmentation process for Speed Disk and Disk Tune, respectively.

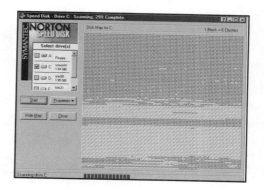

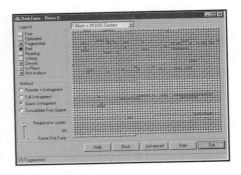

Both programs are very easy to use. After you install the program as part of the suite of utilities, start the program and select the drive (if your PC has more than one disk drive) you want to defragment and simply let the program run.

Depending on how fragmented your files are, how large your hard disk drive is, and the speed of your PC, the defragmentation process can take anywhere from a few minutes to several hours. Just be patient and let the program do its job. If this is the first time you are defragmenting your hard disk drive, you might want to start it late at night and let it run overnight.

After you are familiar with the basic techniques of your defragmenter, you might want to begin using some of its more advanced features, such as directory sorting, file placement, and write verification. All these features are used to either improve efficiency of the disk drive, improve ease of use for you, or to ensure that files, which are rearranged on your disk, are still viable.

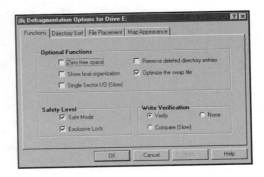

Most defragmentation programs offer these types of advanced features. If you are running Windows NT 4.0 on your PC, there are disk defragmenters that you can run in the background that continuously defragment your hard disk drive.

Cheat Sheet

Creating a Startup Disk in Windows 95/98

1. Exit any programs you have running. Make sure you have a 3 1/2" disk and your Windows 98 installation CD handy before you begin.

2. Insert the 3 1/2" disk into drive A:.

3. From the Start menu, select Settings, Control Panel to open the Windows Control Panel.

4. Double-click the Add/Remove Programs icon to open the Add/Remove Programs Properties dialog box.

5. Select the Startup Disk tab and click the Create Disk button to begin creating your startup disk.

6. When you are prompted, insert your Windows 98 installation CD in your CD-ROM drive so that any files that are needed can be copied to your startup disk.

Creating a Rescue Disk by Using Norton Utilities

1. From the Start menu, select Programs, Norton Utilities, and then select the Rescue Disk icon.

2. After the program starts, select where you want to store your Rescue disk files.

3. Before you begin creating your Rescue disk, click the Options button and select the type of Rescue information you want to save.

4. Click OK, and then click Start to begin creating the Rescue disk.

41

Creating a Startup Disk

You may never need a startup disk for your computer, but think of it like fire insurance—you have it just in case you need it, but hope you never have to use it.

The vast majority of the time, Windows 98 should start up on your PC without a hitch. If Windows 98 should ever fail to boot, either because of a disk error, one of the system files becomes damaged or corrupted, or you accidentally delete one of your system files, you need a startup disk to start your PC and access your files.

A startup disk is a bootable disk that contains a copy of the system files used to start up your PC and provide access to peripheral devices such as CD-ROM or Zip drives.

Basic Survival

Creating a Startup Disk in Windows 95/98

Windows 98 (and its predecessor Windows 95) comes equipped with a program for creating a startup disk. You need one blank 3 1/2" floppy disk and your original Windows 98 installation CD.

Following is the procedure for creating your startup disk:

1. Exit all programs you might have running.

2. Insert a blank 3 1/2" floppy disk into drive A:.

3. From the Start menu, select Settings, Control Panel to open the Windows Control Panel.

4. Double-click the Add/Remove Programs icon to open the Add/Remove Programs Properties dialog box.

Double-click this icon to
create a startup disk.

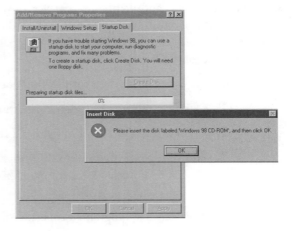

5. Select the Startup Disk tab.

6. Click the Create Disk button to begin creating your start-up disk. When prompted, insert your Windows 98 installation CD.

Be sure to keep your startup disk in a safe place until you need it. If you ever make any changes in your PC, such as adding new programs to your Startup folder or adding/changing any peripheral devices, you need to create a new startup disk to reflect your changes.

Beyond Survival

Creating a Rescue Disk by Using Norton Utilities

In you purchased either Norton Utilities or Nuts & Bolts to use the disk defragmenter portion of the utility suite, you already have a more comprehensive means of creating a Windows start-up disk. Both programs refer to the startup disk as a Rescue disk.

Both programs also allow you to add additional programs to your startup disk in order to perform some diagnostic and repair functions by using utilities from their respective suite of utilities. Norton Utilities allows you to create a Rescue disk that includes more files than fit on a 1.44M floppy disk.

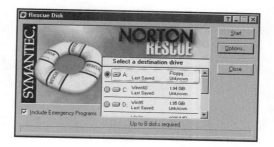

To create a Rescue disk by using Norton Utilities:

1. From the Start menu, select Programs, Norton Utilities, and then select the Rescue Disk icon to start the Rescue Disk utility program.

2. After the program starts, select where you want to store your Rescue disk files. Because the Norton Utilities Rescue disk can work in conjunction with your Windows 98 startup disk, you can store your Rescue disk information on one of your hard disk drives. Remember that if the cause of your startup or boot error is disk (hardware) failure, you may not be able to access any information you store on the affected hard disk drive.

3. Before you begin creating your Rescue disk, click the Options button and select the type of Rescue information you want to save. Your Rescue information can include Norton AntiVirus files (if you also own Norton AntiVirus) and various disk and system utilities from the Norton Utilities disk suite.

Select the information you want to save.

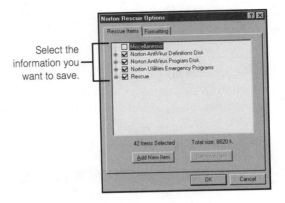

4. After you select the options, click OK and then click Start to begin creating the Rescue disk.

Cheat Sheet

Performing a Backup

1. From the Start menu, select Programs, Accessories, System Tools, and then select Backup to start the Windows 98 Backup utility program.

2. Select the files you want to back up by selecting the check box in front of either a file or folder.

3. After you have selected all the files you want to back up, click the Next Step button.

4. At the next screen, select the device you are backing up to. If you are backing up to a floppy disk in drive A:, select drive A:.

5. After you have selected your backup device, click the Start Backup button to begin your backup.

6. When prompted, supply a name for your backup set. If you desire, you can also supply a password for your backup set.

42

Backing Up Your System

The best insurance against any potential problems to your PC data is a recent backup of your important files. Windows 95/98 comes with a Backup utility program you can use to back up selected files or your entire hard disk drive.

Basic Survival

Performing a Backup

You can use the Backup utility in Windows 98 to selectively back up any files or groups of files on your hard disk drive. In most cases, when you back up files, you are doing your backup to one or more floppy disks or to a slightly larger storage medium such as a Zip disk or a network volume if you are connected to a network.

The following steps show you how to use the Windows 98 Backup utility to back up a group of files to a floppy disk:

1. From the Start menu, select Programs, Accessories, System Tools, and then select Backup to start the Windows 98 Backup utility program.

2. Select the files you want to back up by selecting the check box in front of either a file or folder.

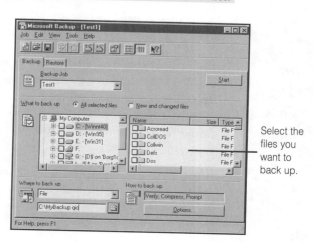

Select the files you want to back up.

3. After you have selected all the files you want to back up, click the Next Step button.

4. At the next screen, select the device you are backing up to. If you are backing up to a floppy disk in drive A:, select drive A:.

5. After you have selected your backup device, click the Start Backup button to begin your backup.

6. When prompted, supply a name for your backup set. If you desire, you can also supply a password for your backup set.

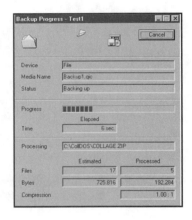

If you select more files than fit on a single floppy disk, Backup prompts you to enter successive disks, as needed.

Beyond Survival

Other Backup Options

Backing up your entire hard disk drive to floppy disks can seem like an endless exercise in futility, especially because the hard disk drives in most PCs these days are in the 2–3GB (gigabyte) range. To back up a 2GB drive onto a 1.44M floppy disk would require more than 1,300 disks and a lot more time than you want to spend swapping floppies.

If you want to back up your entire hard disk drive, you can still use the Backup utility, but you need a storage medium that is up to the task. This means you need to use some type of tape backup device, or one of the large capacity removable media type drives such as the Iomega Jaz drive, Zip drive, or the Syquest removable media drive.

The Backup utility includes options specifically for use with tape drives, such as the following:

- The capability to automatically detect a tape drive

- An option to erase or format a tape in a tape drive

- An option to perform a file verification on the tape contents after the backup

- An option to perform full or incremental backups

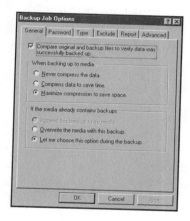

Even though the Windows 98 Backup utility allows you to perform incremental backups, there are several good reasons not to. In theory, incremental backups sound like a good idea—you first perform a full backup and then the next few times you perform your backup, you back up only files that have changed. Sounds like a good idea until you have to restore more than just a few files. If your incremental backups are spread across several tapes, you may have trouble locating the particular tape that stores the file or files you are looking for. My advice is if you can perform a full backup on one tape, then do so and let your backups run overnight.

Cheat Sheet

Restoring Data

1. From the Start menu, select Programs, Accessories, System Tools, and Backup to start the Windows 98 Backup utility program.

2. Select the Restore tab to indicate that you are restoring and not backing up files.

3. Select your restore device, which is the device you backed up your files to. If you backed up to a floppy disk, make sure you load the disk into your drive.

4. Select your backup set on your backup device. Click the Next Step button to continue.

5. If you are not restoring the entire backup set (all the files in the backup set), select the file or files you want to restore.

6. Click the Start Restore button to begin restoring your files.

43

Restoring Your Data from a Backup

In the last chapter, you learned how to perform backups by using the Windows 98 Backup utility, both to floppy disks (when you are backing up only a few files) and to tape or other media (when you need to back up your entire hard disk drive). Well, backups are no good if you can't restore the files you backed up, so in this chapter you see what you need to do to restore the files you just learned to back up.

Basic Survival

Restoring Data

As you might expect, the restore process is the opposite of the backup procedure. Here's how to restore the files you just backed up:

1. From the Start menu, select Programs, Accessories, System Tools, and Backup to start the Windows 98 Backup utility program.

2. Select the Restore tab to indicate that you are restoring and not backing up files.

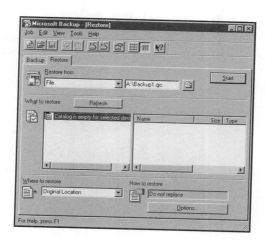

3. Select your restore device, which is the device you backed up your files to. If you backed up to a floppy disk, make sure you load the disk (or if you backed up to more than one disk, load the first disk) into your drive.

4. Select your backup set on your backup device. Click the Next Step button to continue.

5. If you are not restoring the entire backup set (all the files in the backup set), then select the file or files you want to restore.

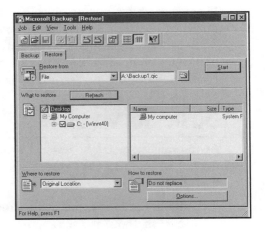

6. Click the Start Restore button to begin restoring your files.

Beyond Survival

Advanced Restore Options

The Windows 98 Backup utility does contain some advanced features, which you can use to better control your file restoration procedure.

To examine the advanced file restore options, use the following steps:

1. From the Start menu, select Programs, Accessories, System Tools, and Backup to start the Windows 98 Backup utility program.

2. Select the Restore tab to indicate that you are restoring, not backing up files.

3. Select Settings to open the Settings menu, and then select Options to open the Settings–Options dialog box.

4. Select the Restore tab to view the Restore options.

Advanced restore options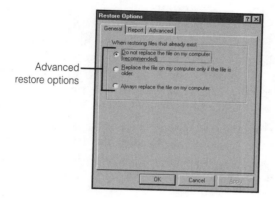

The advanced restore options enable you to do the following:

- Restore your files into different locations (drive and folder) from where you backed them up.

- Verify your file restoration against your backup set.

- Control whether the files (if restored back to the original folder) will or will not overwrite the existing files, or overwrite the files if they are older than the files from your backup set.

Cheat Sheet

Using the Add New Hardware Wizard

1. From the Start menu, select Settings, Control Panel to open the Windows Control Panel.

2. In the Control Panel, double-click the Add New Hardware icon to start the Add New Hardware Wizard.

3. Click the Next button twice to start the wizard.

4. In most cases, the wizard should be able to locate the device on its own. Follow the prompts supplied by the wizard. Try to let the wizard do as much of the search process as it can. If the wizard still cannot locate the new device, when you are prompted select the new device from the list of devices Windows knows how to configure.

5. After the new device has been identified to Windows, the wizard should have no trouble configuring the device. Make sure you have your installation CD handy in case the wizard prompts you to load it so that it can retrieve a device driver.

44

Installing New Hardware

Installing new hardware in your PC has never been easier. Years ago when you wanted to add a device such as a sound card or an internal modem, you had to worry about making sure all the hardware interrupt and memory settings were correct and not being used by an existing device, and whether you had the right hardware device driver installed. Experienced users sometimes took hours to install a new device and inexperienced users simply gave up in disgust or paid someone to install the peripheral device.

Whenever possible, make sure any new devices you purchase are clearly labeled "Plug and Play." Non-Plug and Play devices are commonly called "legacy" devices.

Windows 98 includes a feature called Plug and Play, which makes installing new hardware devices practically as simple as turning on your PC. The Plug and Play feature in Windows 98 (and Windows 95) works with Plug and Play hardware devices and automatically detects what settings are needed by the device and makes all the configuration changes for you. The Windows 98 Plug and Play feature also prompts you to insert your Windows 98 installation CD, download, and install the proper hardware device driver if one is needed.

Basic Survival

Adding New Plug and Play Hardware

In most cases, when you install a new Plug and Play hardware device in your PC, Windows 98 detects the new device when you start up your computer, and begins configuring the device for you. During this configuration, Windows 98 makes sure that the settings it uses for the new device do not conflict with settings on existing hardware devices in your PC. If the new hardware device requires a device driver, Windows prompts you to install your installation CD into your CD-ROM drive and attempts to locate and install the proper device driver.

Beyond Survival

Using the Add New Hardware Wizard

As good as Plug and Play may sound on paper, it is not perfect and occasionally some devices are either not configured properly, Windows is not able to properly identify the device, or Windows is not able to locate the proper device driver for the new peripheral. When this happens, you need to manually run the Add New Hardware Wizard to help jump-start the installation and configuration process.

To run the Add New Hardware Wizard, follow these steps:

1. From the Start menu, select Settings, Control Panel to open the Windows Control Panel.

Double-click this icon to add new hardware.

If you are having trouble getting a new device installed, be sure to check the manufacturer's Web site to see whether a newer device driver has been issued.

2. In the Control Panel, double-click the Add New Hardware icon to start the Add New Hardware Wizard.

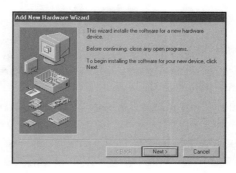

3. Click the Next button twice to start the wizard. The wizard begins by searching for the new hardware device you have installed.

4. In most cases, the wizard should be able to locate the device on its own. But, if it cannot locate the new device, you need to help. Follow the prompts supplied by the wizard. Try to let the wizard do as much of the search process as it can. If the wizard still cannot locate the new device, when you are prompted select the new device from the list of devices Windows knows how to configure.

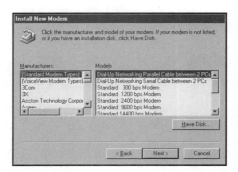

5. After the new device has been identified to Windows, the wizard should have no trouble configuring the device. Make sure you have your installation CD handy in case the wizard prompts you to load it so that it can retrieve a device driver.

Cheat Sheet

Starting the Device Manager

1. From the Start menu, select Settings, Control Panel to open the Windows Control Panel.

2. In the Control Panel, double-click the System icon to open the System Properties dialog box.

3. Select the Device Manager tab to access the Device Manager.

4. In the Device Manager, a red X on a hardware item means that the device has been disabled. A yellow exclamation mark means there is a problem with the device. To see how Device Manager is attempting to diagnose the problem, select the device and then click the Properties button.

45

Troubleshooting Problems

Windows 98 does not provide many tools to help you diagnose problems with your PC. However, there is one tool—the Device Manager—that can provide some basic information on some minor problems with your PC.

Basic Survival

Using the Device Manager

Although the Device Manager is definitely not in the class of "heavy-duty" diagnostic tools, you can use it to spot some simple problems in your PC such as memory or interrupt conflicts with peripheral devices, or when a device driver is not installed or functioning properly.

To use the Device Manager, follow these steps:

1. From the Start menu, select Settings, Control Panel to open the Windows Control Panel.

2. In the Control Panel, double-click the System icon to open the System Properties dialog box.

3. Select the Device Manager tab to access the Device Manager.

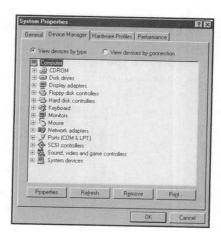

4. In the Device Manager, a red X on a hardware item means that device has been disabled. A yellow exclamation mark means there is a problem with the device. To see how Device Manager is attempting to diagnose the problem, select the device and then click the Properties button.

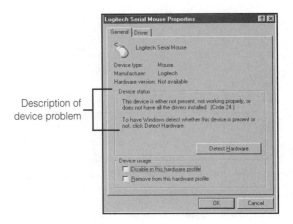

Description of device problem

Beyond Survival

Other Diagnostics Tools

If you're looking for "heavy-duty" diagnostic tools, you may already have installed what you're looking for. If you purchased and installed either the Norton Utilities or Nuts & Bolts program (discussed in Chapter 40, "Defragmenting Your Hard Disk"), you already have a heavy-duty PC diagnostics utility.

Running the Norton Utilities System Doctor

The Norton Utilities includes a module called the System Doctor that can be used to monitor vital systems in your PC and provide you with warnings and alerts on your PC's memory, disks, and other system components.

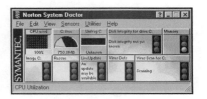

The Norton System Doctor is configurable—meaning you can add or remove whatever sensors you feel you need to monitor your PC. When you install the Norton Utilities, by default the System Doctor is configured to start automatically when you start your PC.

To add additional sensors, use the following steps:

1. Start Norton System Doctor, and select Sensors on the main menu to open the Sensor menu.

2. Select the type of sensor you want to add—Memory, Disk, System, Internet/Network, or Performance.

3. Select the sensor you want to add for the particular operation you want to monitor.

4. Click the Close button to exit the utility.

Running Nuts & Bolts Discover

The Nuts & Bolts utility suite also contains a fairly powerful and comprehensive diagnostics utility program. To launch the utility program, follow these steps:

1. From the Start menu, select Programs, Nuts & Bolts, and select the Nuts & Bolts icon to start the program.

2. Click the Discover button to start the Discover utility program.

3. After Discover starts, select the Diagnostics tab to open the diagnostics portion of Discover.

4. In the check boxes on the right side of the screen, select the diagnostic test you want to run. Click the Test button to begin running the diagnostic program.

Choose the tests
you want to run.

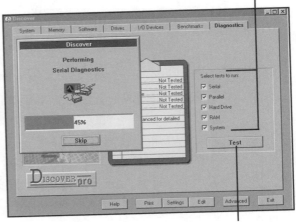

Click here to begin.

5. In a few minutes, the results of the tests are completed; if there are any problems detected, Nuts & Bolts advises what your next course of action should be. If you want to perform more detailed diagnostics, click the Advanced button to proceed to the advanced diagnostics section of Discover, shown in the following figure.

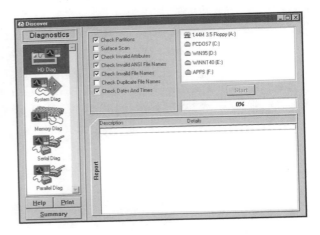

Running SiSoft Sandra

If neither Norton Utilities nor Nuts & Bolts appeals to you, you can purchase another excellent PC diagnostics program over the Internet. Point your browser to www.sisoftware.demon.co.uk/sandra where you find SiSoft Sandra 98.

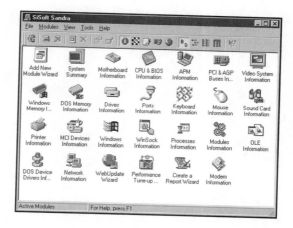

SiSoft Sandra 98 is strictly a diagnostics and configuration utility and it is one of the most detailed PC diagnostics programs available to the general public. If you want more information on the capabilities of this program, go to the SiSoft Web site listed previously.

PART

6

Connecting to the Internet

You are no longer limited to just your office or home and the PC. With your PC and the right equipment, you can connect to the Internet, a network of networks. After connected, you have access to a wealth of information and services. If you have a modem and an Internet connection, read this part to see some of the things you can do. The following topics are covered:

- Getting Connected to the Internet
- Starting and Exiting Internet Explorer
- Browsing the Internet
- Searching the Internet
- Sending and Receiving Email
- Joining Newsgroups

Cheat Sheet

Setting Up for the Internet

1. Click Start, choose Programs, select Internet Explorer, and click Connection Wizard.

2. Select the appropriate setup option, and then click the Next button.

3. Specify how you want to get connected, and then click Next.

4. Select to use an existing dial-up connection or to create a new one, and then click Next.

5. Type the telephone number you use to connect to your Internet Service Provider and click Next.

6. Type your username and the password assigned to you by your ISP, and then click Next.

7. Proceed through the remaining steps of the wizard, providing the information that is requested. Click Next to move on to the next step.

8. Click the Finish button to complete the setup.

46

Getting Connected to the Internet

To get connected to the Internet, you need to have a modem, a phone line (or network connection), and an Internet provider. You also need a browser, a program that enables you to view content and also usually provides mail and newsgroup features. (See Chapter 51, "Joining Newsgroups," for more information on newsgroups.) With all this equipment, you can get set up.

Basic Survival

What You Need to Get Connected

The first thing you need to get connected is a modem. Modem stands for *MO*dulator-*DEM*odulator, which means it translates the digital information (from the PC) to analog (that the phone line can carry), and sends the analog information over the phone lines. The receiving modem then translates the analog information back to digital.

You also need a phone line. You can use your existing phone, but then you have to coordinate when the line is used for the PC and when the line is used for phone calls. You may want to install a second line specifically for your modem. You may also connect through your company's network rather than through the phone lines. (See Part 7, "Networking," for information on networks.)

Consider adding a second phone line for the modem.

In addition to the hardware, you need an Internet Service Provider (ISP). This company provides you with a hookup to its network, usually for a monthly fee. From its network, you can get connected to the Internet. The ISP also provides the necessary programs to browse the Internet, handle email, and read newsgroup messages. (Windows 98 also includes the same set of tools.)

One easy way to get connected to the Internet is through an online service such as America Online (AOL). You can take advantage of all the features of the online service in addition to using it as a gateway to the Internet. You may find, though, that you have trouble connecting with AOL—that is, get a lot of busy signals.

You can also find an independent service provider that focuses just on Internet connections. These may provide additional features, such as helping you publish your own Web page. You can find independent service providers by looking in the Yellow Pages, by asking friends and coworkers for recommendations, or by checking out one of the many Internet directories or magazines for information.

For each of the tasks you do on the Internet, you need a program for handling that particular task. For instance, to browse the World Wide Web, you need a Web browser. To read and send email messages, you need an email program. To participate in newsgroups, you need a newsreader.

Usually your Internet Service Provider provides the necessary software. You can also use two popular programs, Netscape Communicator and Internet Explorer (included with Windows), to access the Internet. Both of these programs are really a complete suite of Internet tools and include all the programs you need to browse, send mail, transfer files, join newsgroups, and so on.

Setting Up for the Internet

After you have all the equipment and connections, you need to get set up. Windows makes it easy to set up by providing a wizard. The following steps lead you through the entire wizard, and include setting up a new Internet account, mail account, and newsgroup account. If you already have an account, select that option and follow the onscreen instructions. If you don't want to set up a particular account, you can skip it. You can run the wizard again to set up the accounts you didn't set up the first time.

The following steps give you the basic procedure in Windows 98, but if you make different choices, the steps may vary. Simply follow the wizard's instructions.

Follow these steps to set up for the Internet for the first time:

1. Click Start, choose Programs, select Internet Explorer, and click Connection Wizard.

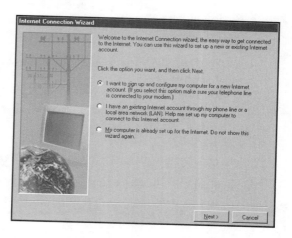

2. If you don't already have an Internet provider and want to find one and set up an account, select the first option and then click Next. Follow the wizard's directions.

If you have an existing account and want to set up your PC for this account, select the second option and then click Next. (These steps cover how to set up the PC for an existing account.)

Click the Help button in any wizard dialog box for more detailed instructions.

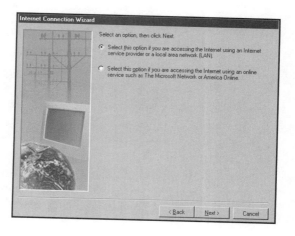

3. Specify whether you want to connect through an Internet Service Provider or LAN, or through an online service. Click Next.

Click the Back button if you need to go back through your choices and make a change.

4. Select how to get connected—through the phone line or LAN. For information on networks (LANs), see Part 7, "Networking," of this book. Click Next.

5. Select the modem you want to use to get connected and click Next.

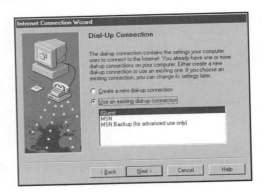

6. Select to use an existing dial-up connection or create a new one, and then click Next.

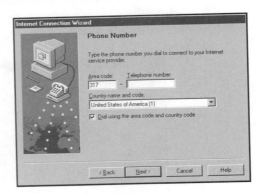

7. If you select to create a new dial-up connection, type the telephone number you use to connect to your Internet Service Provider and click Next.

8. Type your username and the password assigned to you by your ISP, and then click Next.

9. If you do not want to change the advanced settings, click No and then click Next. For the most part, you shouldn't need to change these settings.

10. Type a name for your dial-up connection—any name you want—and then click Next.

11. Select Yes if you want to set up your Internet mail account, and then click Next.

12. If you selected to set up a mail account, specify whether you want to use an existing account or to create a new account and then click Next.

13. To create a new account, type the name you want displayed in messages and then click Next. Type the email address assigned to you by your ISP, and then click Next.

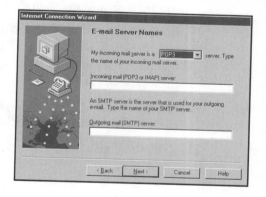

14. Enter the requested information about your incoming and outgoing mail servers (you can get this information from your ISP), and then click Next.

15. Specify logon instructions, and then click Next. Type a name for the mail account, and then click Next.

16. Select Yes if you want to set up a news account and click Next.

17. Specify whether you want to use an existing account or to create a new account, and then click Next.

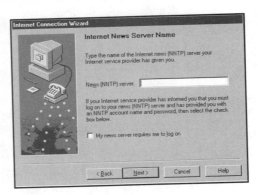

18. If you selected to create a new account, type the name you want displayed in messages posted to the newsgroup, and then click Next. Type the email address assigned to you by your ISP, and then click Next.

19. Enter the requested information about your news server and then click Next. Your ISP should provide this information. Type a name to identify the news account, and then click Next.

20. Select No when prompted to set up an Internet directory service account, and then click Next.

21. Click the Finish button to complete the setup.

Cheat Sheet

Logging On

1. Double-click the Internet icon.
2. When prompted, sign on to your Internet provider.

Logging Off

1. To exit the browser, click the Close button in the upper-right corner of the browser window.
2. Right-click the Internet connection icon in the status bar and choose Disconnect to end your ISP connection.

47

Starting and Exiting Internet Explorer

After you've got your Internet connection set up, you can start Internet Explorer and browse the Internet. If you have problems connecting—the line is busy, for instance—try again. If you continue to have problems, check with your ISP.

Basic Survival

Logging On

Your Internet provider gives you specific instructions for how to log on to the Internet. Following are the basic steps:

1. Double-click the Internet icon. (Usually the installation program sets up an icon for Internet access.)

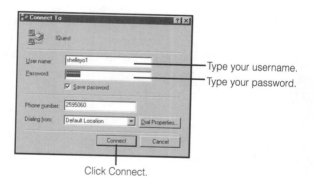

Type your username.
Type your password.

Click Connect.

2. When prompted, sign on to your Internet provider. Normally, you type your username and password.

When you connect, you see your home page, which varies depending on which browser you are using. The following shows Internet Explorer and the start page for this browser, usually the Microsoft home page.

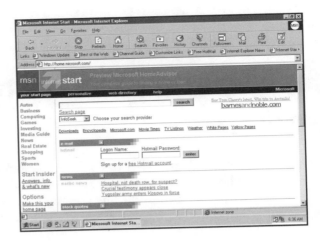

Logging Off

When you are finished browsing the Internet, you need to exit Internet Explorer and also end your connection to your Internet provider. Follow these steps:

1. To exit the browser, click the Close button in the upper-right corner of the browser window.

2. You may be prompted to disconnect from your ISP. If you are, click the OK or Yes button to disconnect. If you are not prompted, you can disconnect by right-clicking on the Internet connection icon in the status bar and choosing Disconnect.

Cheat Sheet

Using Links to Explore the Internet

1. Click the link on the Web page.
2. Continue clicking links until you find the information you want.

Typing an Address

1. Click in the Address text box.
2. Type the address you want to go to and press Enter.

Adding a Site to Your Favorites List

1. Go to the page you want to add.
2. Open the Favorites menu and select the Add to Favorites command.
3. Type a name for the page and then click OK.

Going to a Site in Your Favorites List

1. Click the Favorites button on the toolbar.
2. Click the site you want to visit.

Using the History List

1. Click the History button in the toolbar.
2. If necessary, select the week whose list you want to review.
3. Click the site you want.

48

Browsing the Internet

Everything on the Web is displayed as a document page. Web pages can contain text, graphics, sounds, movies, and links to other Web pages. These links are what make it possible to browse the Web. When you click a link, you're taken to another page on the Web, which contains information as well as other links. Not only can you review the information and pictures on each page, but you can also click any of the links to get additional information.

This chapter describes how to browse the Internet—by using links, typing addresses, and clicking the toolbar buttons.

Basic Survival

Clicking Links to Browse

Information on the Internet is easy to browse because documents contain *links* to other pages, documents, and sites. Simply click a link to view the associated page. A link may take you to another page in that document, to another document at that site, or to an entirely new site. The journey is half the fun! Links usually appear underlined; images also may be links. You can tell whether an image (or text) is a link by placing your mouse pointer on it. If the pointer changes into a pointing hand, the image (or text) is a link.

Links usually appear under-lined and in a different color.

If you see an error message when you click a link, it could indicate that the link is not accurate or that the server is busy. Try again later.

To navigate from page to page by using links, follow these steps:

1. **From any Web page, click the link.** For instance, you can click any of the links on the Amazon.com page (an online bookstore) shown in the following figure.

2. Continue clicking links until you find the information you want.

Typing an Address

Each Web page has a unique address called a URL or uniform resource locator. For example, here's the URL for the White House:

```
http://www.whitehouse.gov
```

The first part is the protocol (usually **http://** and then **www** for Web pages). Next, you have the domain name (**whitehouse**) and then the extension (usually **.com**, **.net**, **.gov**, **.edu**, or **.mil**), which indicates the type of site (commercial, network resources, government, educational, or military, respectively). You can find addresses in advertisements, articles, books, and so on.

Typing a site's address is the fastest way to get to that site. Follow these steps:

1. Click in the Address text box near the top of the screen. The entire address of the current page should be highlighted.

Type the address here.

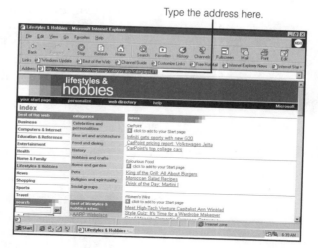

2. Type the address you want to go to and press Enter. You see that page.

Using Toolbar Buttons

When you click a link or type an address, you journey from page to page. To help you navigate among the pages, you can also use the buttons in the toolbar. You can go back to pages you have previously viewed, forward through pages after going back, and back to your start page. Do any of the following:

• Click the Back button to go back to a page you previously viewed.

• If you have gone back, you can also go forward. Click the Forward button to move forward through the pages you've already visited.

• To return to the Microsoft start page, click the Home button in the toolbar.

Beyond Survival

Adding a Site to Your Favorites List

When you find a site that you especially like, you might want a quick way to return to it without having to browse from link to link or having to remember the address. You can add the page to a list of favorite sites.

Internet Explorer uses the term *Favorites* and displays the items in folders. If you use another browser, you may follow a different procedure. For instance, Netscape Navigator (included with Netscape Communicator) uses *bookmarks*. Use the Bookmarks menu in Netscape to add and go to bookmarks.

To add a site to your Favorites list, follow these steps:

1. Go to the page you want to add.

2. Open the Favorites menu and select the Add To Favorites command.

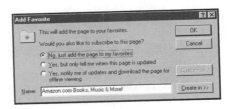

3. Type a name for the page (or keep the default name) and then click OK.

Going to a Site in Your Favorites List

After you have added a site to your Favorites list, you can easily reach that site by displaying the list and selecting the site. Follow these steps to go to a site in your Favorites list:

1. Click the Favorites button on the toolbar. The pane on the left side of the screen contains your Favorites list, whereas the right pane contains the current page.

Favorites list

2. Click the site you want to visit. You see that page.

3. To close the Favorites bar, click its Close (X) button.

Using the History List

As you browse from link to link, you might remember a site that you liked, but not remember that site's name or address. You can easily return to sites you have visited. In both Internet Explorer and Netscape Navigator, you display the History list, but the procedure is a little different for Netscape Navigator. To view the History list in Netscape, you choose Window, History.

To view a history list in Internet Explorer, follow these steps:

1. Click the History button in the toolbar. You see the History list in a pane on the left side of the window.

History list

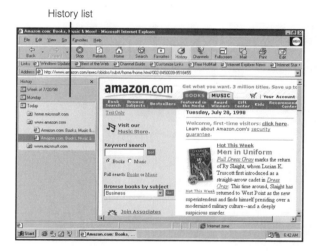

2. If necessary, select the week whose list you want to review.

3. Click the site you want. Internet Explorer displays that site.

4. To close the History bar, click its Close (X) button.

Cheat Sheet

Searching the Internet

1. Click the Search button in your browser's toolbar.
2. Select the search engine you want to use.
3. In the text box, type the word or phrase you want to find.
4. Click the Search button.
5. To go to any of the found sites, click the link to that site.

49

Searching the Internet

Browsing around the Internet is time-consuming (but fun). You never know where you're going to end up. You might start out researching a legitimate project and end up checking out pictures of bulldogs on the bulldog page. When you have an idea of what you want to find and want to see what's available, you can search for specific topics on the Web.

Basic Survival

Searching the Internet

To search the Internet, you use a search engine, and there are many different search engines available. They all work basically the same: You type the word or phrase you want to find and click the search button. The search engine then displays matches. (You also can fine-tune the search by using different search options.)

The search tools differ in how they search—where they look for matches for your words. That means the results vary. Also, how the results are displayed varies. Some display a short description. Some include some indication of how well the listed site matches the criteria you entered. Some may provide reviews of sites.

Follow these steps to search for topics on the Internet:

1. Click the Search (or Find) button in your browser's toolbar. You see a list of the different search engines from which you can select.

2. Select the search engine you want to use. To select a different search engine in Internet Explorer, click the Select provider drop-down list and click the tool you want to use.

Type what you
want to find.

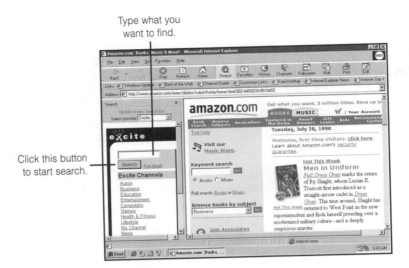

Click this button
to start search.

3. In the text box, type the word or phrase you want to find
   and then click the Search button. (The name of the button varies depending on which search engine you use.)
   You see the results of the search—a list of possible
   matches.

Search
results

4. To go to any of the found sites, click the link to that site.
   If additional sites were found, you can also display the
   next set of sites. Look for a link at the end of the list to
   display the next set of matches.

Beyond Survival

Using Search Page Directories

If you don't find the topic you want, you can try a different search engine. The results may be different.

Search engines include features to help you navigate throughout the vast amount of information available on the Internet. Many search engines provide directories or channels. You can browse these channels to find topics of interest.

For instance, Infoseek, one of the most popular search engines, includes the following topics: Automotive, Business, Careers, Education, Health, Kids & Family, and others. To view the sites in these categories, click the link. Then click any of the links within that category.

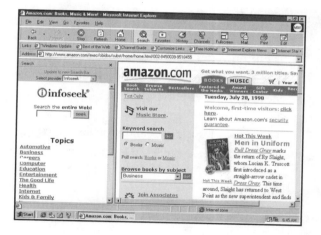

Excite, another popular search engine, includes similar channels (Autos, Business, Education, Entertainment, Lifestyle, and so on). Again, click the channel and then click the link you want to visit.

Cheat Sheet

Starting Your Email Program

1. Log on to your Internet Service Provider.
2. Start the email program.

Checking Your Mail

1. Start your email program.
2. Check for new messages.
3. To read a message, double-click it.

Sending New Mail

1. In your email program, click the New Message button. (The name of this button varies from program to program.)
2. In the To text box, type the address of the recipient.
3. Type a short description or header for the message in the Subject field.
4. Click in the message area and type your message.
5. To send the message, click the Send button.

Responding to Mail

1. Display the message to which you want to reply.
2. Click the Reply button or select the Reply command. (The name of this command varies from program to program.)
3. Type your response and click the Send button.

50

Sending and Receiving Email

If you are connected to the Internet, you can send messages to colleagues, clients, friends, and family, and you can read and reply to messages others send you. To use the email features of the Internet, you need to have a program that can handle email. You may use the program provided by your Internet Service Provider, or you may use the integrated email programs included with Microsoft's Internet Explorer (Outlook Express Mail) or Netscape Communicator (Netscape Messenger). As another alternative, you may use an online service such as America Online for your mail. Finally, you may purchase and use another email package.

Most email programs offer comparable features and work in a similar fashion. The exact steps you follow to access mail and send and receive mail vary from program to program. This chapter uses Outlook Express as the mail program.

Basic Survival

Starting Your Email Program

To check your mail, you first log on to your Internet Service Provider and then start the mail program. The process varies depending on which program you use. Usually you start the mail program as you do any other program: with a command or program icon.

When you install your email program, that program may put an icon on the desktop. You can double-click this icon to start your mail program.

If you aren't sure, check the information you received from your service provider.

After you start your mail program, you see the program window. The following figure shows the mail window for Outlook Express. If you use another program, your mail program looks a little different, but should contain similar features.

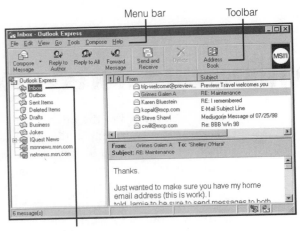

Menu bar   Toolbar

Inbox

Expect to find a menu bar with commands for accessing all the mail features. Most programs also include a toolbar with buttons you can use as shortcuts to common tasks such as checking mail or creating a new message.

Most programs list the message headers in the window. This line tells you the sender, subject, and receive date. You can also usually tell which messages have been read and which have not. For instance, in Outlook Express, bold messages have not been read.

The program window may be divided into panes, like Outlook Express. The left pane lists the folders for handling and storing mail (and also newsgroups). The top-right pane contains message headers, and the bottom-right pane displays the contents of the selected message.

Understanding Your Email Address

To receive mail, you must have an email address, and this address is assigned to you by your Internet Service Provider. Usually you can select your username, which often is the first part of your email address. Following is an example of an address:

username@provider.net

The first part is a username, and the second part defines the server or Internet provider where the mail is sent. Again, check the information sent to you by your ISP to find out your email address.

Checking Your Mail

To check your mail, start the email program, check the mail, and review any messages in your Inbox. Following are the basic steps:

1. **Start your email program.**

2. **Check for new messages.** Some programs may check automatically when you start the program. For others, you may have to select a command (or click a shortcut button) to check the mail. You may also have to type a password.

   Your mail program collects all the messages on your mail server and displays them in your Inbox.

3. **To read a message, double-click it.** You see the contents of the message in a separate message window.

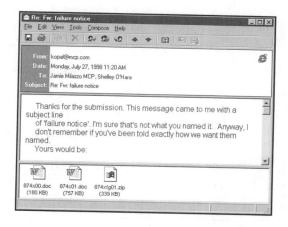

The message window usually includes buttons and commands for handling the message (covered later in this chapter).

Sending New Mail

You aren't limited to just responding to mail you receive. You can also send an email message to any person with an address. Follow these steps:

1. **In your email program, click the New Message button.** (The name of this button varies from program to program.) You can also use a menu command. In Outlook Express, select Compose, New Message. You see a new message window.

Type address   Type subject

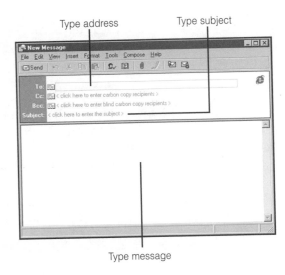

Type message

2. In the To text box, type the address of the recipient. You can also send a carbon copy and blind carbon copy to other recipients by entering addresses in these fields.

3. Type a short description or header for the message in the Subject field.

4. Click in the message area and type your message.

5. To send the message, click the Send button.

You may have other options for sending, depending on the program you are using. For instance, you can assign a priority to the message, attach a file, request a return receipt, and so on.

Most programs enable you to add names to an address book. You can then select them from this list rather than type them.

Responding to Mail

You can easily respond to a message you've received. Most programs complete the address and subject lines for you; you can then simply type the response. Follow these steps:

1. Display the message to which you want to reply.

2. Click the Reply button or select the Reply command. (The name of this command varies from program to program.) You see a message reply window. When you reply, the address information is complete. The reply may also contain the text of the original message.

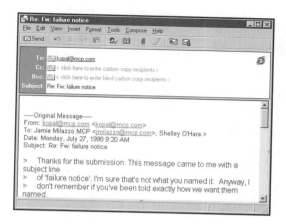

3. Type your response and click the Send button to send the reply.

Beyond Survival

Handling Mail

When you receive a message, you have several choices of what to do with the message:

- **Read and close the message.** To close the message and keep it in your Inbox, click the Close (X) button for the message window.

- **Print the message.** To print the message, look for a Print button in the toolbar or a Print command in the File menu.

- **Delete the message.** To delete the message, use the Delete button in the toolbar.

- **Forward the message.** To forward the message to another person, click the Forward button or use the Forward command. In the To text box, type the address of that person and then click the Send button.

Shortcut: Click the Print button to print a message.

Cheat Sheet

Subscribing to Newsgroups

1. Start your newsreader program.
2. Click the Newsgroups button or open the Tools menu and select Newsgroups.
3. Select the news server you want to use.
4. In the newsgroups list, click the newsgroup you want to join and click the Subscribe button.
5. Continue subscribing to the newsgroups of interest.
6. When you've added all the newsgroups you want, click the OK button.

Reading Newsgroup Messages

1. From the news window, select the newsgroup you want to review.
2. To read a message, click the name in the list.

Replying to a Message

1. To reply to an existing message, select that message in the newsreader window.
2. Click the Reply to Group button. (The name of the button varies. You also can use a menu command.)
3. Click in the message area and type your reply.
4. Click the Post Message button to post the message.

Posting a New Message

1. In the newsreader window, select the group to which you want to post the message.
2. Click the New Message button (or a similarly named button).
3. Type a subject in the Subject line.
4. Click in the message area and type your message.
5. Click the Post Message button.

Joining Newsgroups

A newsgroup is an online discussion group. Each newsgroup is devoted to a particular topic, and you can find newsgroups on topics ranging from current events to Elvis sightings, and from engineering to classical music. There are more than 40,000 newsgroups. The collection of all newsgroups is known as USENET.

You can subscribe to newsgroups of interest and then review and post messages to join in an online discussion. To subscribe to and review newsgroup postings, you need a newsreader. You may have received a news reader program from your Internet Service Provider. Or you can use the newsreader included with Internet Explorer (Outlook Express News) or Netscape Communicator (Netscape Collabra).

Basic Survival

Subscribing to Newsgroups

To read the messages and participate in the newsgroup, you subscribe to the groups you want. The process varies from one program to another, but following are the steps for Outlook Express:

1. Start your newsreader program. To start Outlook Express, click Start, Programs, and Outlook Express.

2. Select your newsreader in the mail window.

3. Click the Newsgroups button or open the Tools menu and select Newsgroups. (The button you click and command you select vary if you are using a different program. Look for something similar.)

4. Select the news server you want to use. You may be able to choose from several news servers. You should see the newsgroups in that server listed.

If this is the first time you are subscribing, you may be prompted to download the complete list. You can also display All newsgroups or all new newsgroups by using the buttons in the dialog box.

Select newsgroup to join.

Click this button to subscribe.

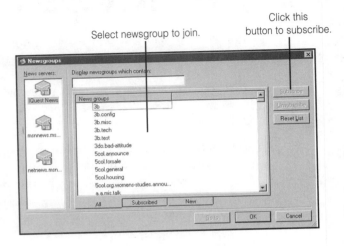

5. In the newsgroups list, click the newsgroup you want to join and click the Subscribe button.

6. Continue subscribing to the newsgroups of interest.

7. When you've added all the newsgroups you want, click the OK button.

Reading Newsgroup Messages

After you have subscribed to a newsgroup, you can review any of the posted messages. Follow these steps:

1. From the news window, select the newsgroup you want to review. In Outlook Express, the newsgroups are listed in the left pane of the window. (You may have to expand the listing to see all the groups within a certain news server.) To select the newsgroup you want, click it.

Outlook Express retrieves the messages. Messages that have replies posted to them are marked with a plus sign. You can expand this list to see all the replies by clicking the plus sign.

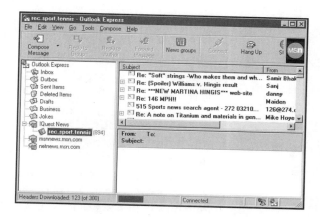

2. To read a message, click the name in the list. You see the message.

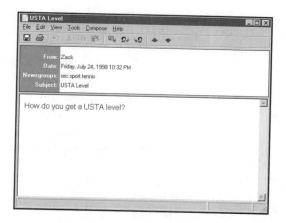

You can review other messages, select other newsgroups, post replies (covered next), or exit the program. To exit, click the Close (X) button for the newsreader.

When you are reviewing messages, keep in mind that messages are often replies from a previous posting. You may not understand the message you are reviewing because you haven't seen the earlier messages. It's kind of like walking in on the middle of a conversation. If the earlier messages are not posted, you have to guess the gist of the message in some cases.

Spend some time reviewing the content of a newsgroup before jumping in.

Also, don't expect to find top-notch quality writing or comments in every posting. You might find that you have to spend some time finding a "good" conversation.

The messages in these newsgroups are not screened for objectionable content. If you find something offensive, the best thing to do is just unsubscribe from that newsgroup.

Replying to a Message

Reviewing posted messages gives you an idea of the content and participants in a newsgroup. You may want to lurk around and read messages to get a feel for the atmosphere. When you are ready, you can post your own replies. Again, the steps vary depending on which newsreader you use, but the basic process is similar.

Follow these steps to post a reply to an existing message using Outlook Express News:

1. To reply to an existing message, select that message in the newsreader window.

2. Click the Reply to Group button. (The name of the button varies. You also can use a menu command.) You see a reply window with the contents of the original posting. The newsgroup is already completed for the To field.

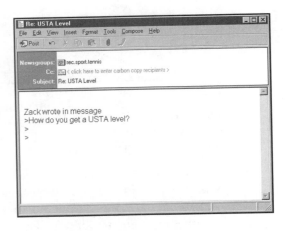

3. Click in the message area and type your reply.

4. Click the Post Message button to post the message.

Beyond Survival

Posting a New Message

You aren't limited to joining existing "conversations." When a new message is posted, it starts a thread, and all responses are part of this thread. You can also start your own thread by posting a new message. Follow these steps to post a new message to a newsgroup:

1. In the newsreader window, select the group to which you want to post the message.

2. Click the New Message button (or a similarly named button). You can also look for a New Message command. You see a new message window, with the current newsgroup entered in the To field.

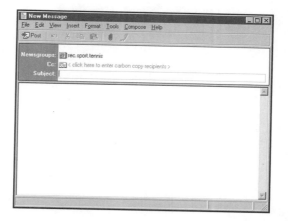

3. Type a subject in the Subject line. This line identifies your message in the newsgroup window, so use something descriptive.

4. Click in the message area and type your message.

5. Click the Post Message button. The message is posted to the newsgroup for others to read and reply to.

If you change your mind about posting a message, you can cancel the message if you have not already clicked the Post Message button. Simply click the message's Close (X) button and, when prompted, click the Yes button to confirm that you don't want to save the message. If you have already clicked the Post Message button, you cannot stop the message.

PART 7

Networking

If you work at a medium to large corporation, there is an excellent chance you have a computer on your desk, and just as good a chance that that computer is connected to your corporation's network. Networks and business seem to go together like bacon and eggs, ham and beans, Abbott and Costello. The purpose of this part is not to make you the next corporate networking guru, but to give you a basic understanding of what's going on behind the scenes of your network and hopefully make you a better corporate network citizen. Some of the topics that are covered in this part include the following:

- Networks Defined

- Hardware Components

- Software Components

- Accessing Your Network and Its Peripherals

- Potential Network Problems

Cheat Sheet

Logging In to Your Network

1. Turn on your PC to start the LAN login procedure, or if your network administrator has otherwise instructed you, start your login procedure.
2. When you are prompted, enter your LAN ID and press Tab.
3. When you are prompted, enter your LAN password and press Enter.

Network Terminology

- **Local area network** A collection of PCs connected together to share resources.
- **Login** A procedure for gaining access to the resources on your network. On most networks, you enter an ID and password to verify your identity when you log in.
- **File server** The central computer on a network that runs the network operating system and controls what type of access each user is granted.
- **Network operating system** A series of programs running on the network file server that control access rights to the various shared resources.
- **Ethernet and Token-Ring** The two major types of networks still used in most businesses.
- **Wide area network** A series of local area networks in different locations connected together.

Networks Defined

Although networks still aren't a very common item in most homes, they are fairly ubiquitous in most businesses. A network is essentially an electronic means of connecting PCs together so that they can share resources. The resources they most often share over networks are disk space, printers, and Internet access.

LAN stands for Local Area Network.

You should also be aware that a network is rarely called a network. Networks are usually referred to as LANs, which is short for Local Area Networks.

Basic Survival

Logging In to Your Network

Most LANs require you to log in before you can access any of the shared resources. When you log in, you usually are required to enter some type of login ID and a password. These requirements are part of the LAN's security system. Most LANs employ some type of security system. Even though the purpose of a LAN is to allow you to share resources with other LAN users, the LAN's security system allows you to keep private and secure any files you create and store on the LAN's shared disk space.

Most PCs connected to a LAN are configured to automatically start the network login procedure when you turn on your PC. Following is a brief example of how to log in to your LAN:

1. Turn on your PC to start the LAN login procedure, or if your network administrator has otherwise instructed you, start your login procedure.

Enter your LAN ID.

Enter your password.

2. When you are prompted, enter your LAN ID and press Tab.

3. When you are prompted, enter your LAN password and press Enter.

If you entered your LAN ID and password correctly, in a few seconds, or a few minutes depending on the procedure for connecting you to your network's shared resources, you should be logged in and ready to begin work.

Logging Out

It's very important that whenever you finish using your PC and want to sever communications with your LAN, you log out properly. The logout procedure can vary depending on what type of network operating system is installed on your LAN and which operating system you are running on your PC. Your network administrator can provide you with the instructions for logging out.

Be sure to log out of the network when you're done using your computer.

Logging out is important because it closes and saves any files you might be working on and signals the file server that you are terminating your network connection. If you do not log out properly, some networks hold your connection open for a period of time even though your PC is turned off. This can adversely affect network performance.

Beyond Survival

Other Network Terminology

How you access your LAN's shared resources depends on how much and the type of access granted to you by your network administrator, what are called your *access rights*. Primarily your administrator sets your access rights to permit or restrict your access to various files and directories on your network file server. Depending on the size of your LAN and how many users there are, your administrator sets up one or more file servers.

A file server is a computer similar to the one sitting on your desk, except that the file server is much more powerful. The file server usually has a lot more memory and disk storage space. The file server also runs a series of programs, called the network operating system. The network operating system allows access to the LAN by the users and controls what resources they are permitted to access. The two major players in the network operating system arena are Novell, which manufactures NetWare, and Microsoft, which manufactures the Microsoft Network (the Windows NT network, not the online service). Chances are the network in your company is using one of these two network operating systems.

Types of Networks

There are mainly two basic types of networks—Ethernet and Token-Ring. In the past, there were several other types, but they all have pretty much fallen by the wayside. The differences between Ethernet and Token-Ring are fairly technical, and as a user you really don't need to concern yourself with these differences.

Some networks use the term directories whereas others use the term folders. For the most part, these terms are interchangeable.

Ethernet was invented first, but for a while *Token-Ring*, invented by IBM, seemed to be making a lot of headway in the corporate world. Ethernet now seems to be the dominant network type mainly because it is cheaper and often easier to implement, and because it offers much faster transmission speeds—100 megabits per second for Ethernet versus 16 megabits per second for Token-Ring.

Networks are not merely confined to one building or area in a company. It is not uncommon for companies that have multiple buildings or locations in a city to have their networks connected. Networks can also be connected over much greater distances such as in different cities. Networks of this type are called WANs, which stands for Wide Area Networks.

Cheat Sheet

Hardware Required for Most Networks

- **Network interface card** An electronic interface card used to connect a computer to a network.
- **Network cable** Category 5, twisted-pair cable is the cable of choice now used in most networks. It is an unshielded cable comprised of 4 pairs of copper wires twisted together.
- **File server** A computer used to control the flow of data and access to network resources.
- **Network hub** An electronic device used to connect the various hardware components of a network. Small network hubs usually contain from 4 to 24 connection ports. Network cables are plugged in to the ports and connect to the various computers and other network hardware devices.
- **Routers and bridges** Electronic communications devices used to separate and segment large networks.

53

Hardware Components

Hardware components for your network can either be very simple or fairly complex, depending on the size and nature of your network.

Basic Survival

You need at least two PCs to form a network. To connect the two PCs, you need at least two network interface cards and a medium for allowing the two PCs to communicate with each other. In the past, that communications medium was some type of cable, but now it is possible to network PCs together using what are called "wireless" LANs. Instead of a cable, the PCs communicate by using radio waves. But the majority of LANs still use cable, some type of copper wire connecting the PCs.

Every PC connected to a network needs to have a network interface card (NIC) installed. The network interface card is an electronic circuit card installed in your PC, which allows your PC to communicate with the rest of the network. Because there are basically two types of networks, Ethernet and Token-Ring, there are also two basic types of network interface cards that are specific to each type of network. You cannot use an Ethernet network interface card on a Token-Ring network or vice versa.

Next comes the network cable that connects each PC, via the card, to the network. The first Ethernet cables were coaxial (coax)—very similar to the coax cable used to bring cable TV to your living room. First, there was thick coax cable, which is about the size of a thin garden hose. Then came thin coax cable that was about the same size as the coax cable used for cable TV. The first Token-Ring cable was about the size of thick Ethernet. It was a thick, heavy, electrically shielded cable.

Now both Ethernet and Token-Ring use what is called Category 5 twisted-pair cable. The cable is similar to the cable used for connecting telephone lines in your home except that instead of two pairs (four wires) of wires twisted together there are four pairs (eight wires) in each cable. The cable is also an unshielded cable, which makes it cheaper, lighter, and easier to work with, but more susceptible to electrical interference—so care must be taken to make sure it is not located near electrical motors or fluorescent lights.

For a PC network, you also need a file server. Some network administrators have gotten away with simply taking a PC, adding extra memory and disk storage space, and designating that PC as their file server. In some cases, when you have a small number of users and the demands on the network are not excessive, you can get way with beefing up a PC and turning it into a file server. But, on larger LANs (that is, 100+ users), you need to use a computer designed specifically to operate as a network file server.

And finally, for a small, simple network you need a small, simple network hub to connect everything together. A hub is what you plug the cables into from each computer. The hub is the device that controls communications between all the computers. Hubs used on small, simple networks typically have anywhere from 4 to 24 plug-in ports used to connect computers.

Beyond Survival

Additional Hardware Required for Larger Networks

For larger, more complex networks with several hundred users in multiple locations, you require additional hardware.

First, you need more file servers. File servers run the network operating system and store the files and programs that network users run on the LAN. There are no hard and fast rules on how many users each file server can accommodate. Most LAN administrators try to limit file servers to between 100–200 users. To accommodate more users, administrators add more memory and disk storage space. Some file servers also allow administrators to add additional CPUs (processors) to handle increases in network demands.

Next, you want to switch from the small, simple hubs used on smaller networks to the larger, manageable-type hubs. Manageable hubs are quite literally hubs with small computers built in that allow administrators to monitor and control the flow of data passing through them. Manageable hubs are also more likely to have a greater capacity for the number of computers and network devices (such as printers, plotters, and scanners) that can be connected into them.

Other hardware devices you are likely to find on larger, more complex networks are *routers and bridges.* These devices are used to help divide large networks in smaller, more manageable segments.

If your network is like most networks and provides email service, you also need additional hardware devices to provide this service. Email is a service that generally runs on a file server set up to act as a type of electronic post office. *Email servers,* as they are called, generally can accommodate somewhere between several hundred and several thousand email users. Each user is also usually provided a mailbox on the server, where incoming email messages are stored until the users read them. The email server is also responsible for forwarding email messages created by users to their intended destination.

Cheat Sheet

Network Software Components

The software used by PCs on a network is generally divided into two distinct areas:

- Server-based software operating on the various network file servers
- Client-based software that runs on the users' PCs

In addition to these minimum software components, some networks also have software for the following functions:

- Database operations
- File backup and restore operations
- Office automation applications
- Electronic mail
- Internet access

Open Windows Firewall — Start - Control Pan
Network & Internet Connections
Windows, Firewall

To Enable Security logging options

Open Windows Firewall
Advanced. Security logging setting

- logging of unsuccessful inbound connec
select - Log dropped packets
- logging of successful Outbound connect
select Log Successful connections

54

Software Components

In the last chapter, you learned about some of the most common hardware components used in the construction of networks. But, you just don't connect all the hardware pieces together and expect your network to start functioning. There are software components you need to add to the mix before anything starts working.

Server-based software controls login operations and security while administering file and print services. Client-based software is used to connect to the network and log in each user. It is also used to access various network resources, such as network drives and network printers.

On the PC side, you need to add two basic programs—a *software driver* to allow your PC to use the network card, and a *network client program* to allow your PC to communicate with the rest of the network.

On the network side, the vast majority of the software for running the network resides on the file server. As was mentioned in the previous chapter, each file server runs a series of programs called the network operating system.

Basic Survival

Network Software Components

There's really not much you can do with your network interface card driver or the network client software running on your PC. Your network administrator or other network technician installs both.

The network interface driver is a program provided by the manufacturer of your network interface card and has the following characteristics:

- Specific to your network card

- Specific to the manufacturer of the network you are connecting to (such as Novell or Microsoft)

- Specific to the type of network you are connected to (such as Ethernet or Token-Ring)

- Specific to the operating system (such as DOS, Windows 95/98, or Windows NT) you are running on your PC

Your network client software is specific to the operating system you are running on your PC and to the manufacturer of the network you are connected to. Your client software allows you to connect to, or log in to, your network. It also allows you to access various network resources depending on the access rights you have been given by your LAN administrator. The most common network resources are disk storage space on one or more file servers and network printers.

Your client software allows you to connect to, or "map" to a directory on your file server and make it appear to be just another hard disk drive.

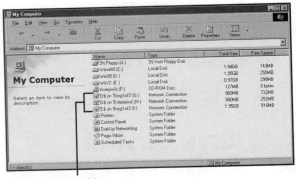

Network drives

Your client software also allows you to connect to multiple network printers the same as if they were directly connected to your PC.

Beyond Survival

Additional Network Software

Most of the software used to operate a network, called the network operating system (NOS), is running on one or more file servers. The network operating system is responsible for controlling numerous activities on the network, such as the following:

- Maintaining security by controlling which users have access to which network resources.

- Permitting and/or regulating access to network resources, such as files and printers, by network users.

- Permitting users to simultaneously run programs installed on file servers.

- Controlling printing and print jobs.

In addition to security and the usual file and print services, file servers are sometimes used to run additional network operations. Some of these additional operations include the following:

- **File backup**   Making a backup copy of the files on your file server in the event that files are damaged or accidentally erased.

- **Communication bridging or routing**   Using a file server with several network cards installed to segment large networks and direct network communication traffic.

- **Email service**   File servers are often used as electronic post offices, providing email service to network users.

- **Database server**   File servers are also used to control large databases.

- **Application servers**   On some very large networks, application programs are distributed along multiple servers instead of residing on the file server used for user login.

Cheat Sheet

Keeping Your Password Secure

- Don't use common names such as nicknames, children's names, or pets' names as your password.
- Use a combination of letters and numbers in your password such as `clarinet23` or `sunshine47`.
- Try to use characters other than letters or numbers in your password, such as `dollar$bird` or `july#56`.
- Don't use birth dates or Social Security numbers as passwords.
- Try to combine unrelated words as passwords, such as `bird%square` or `blue@bovine`.
- Don't reuse old passwords.
- Change your password at least every 30 days.

55

Accessing Your Network and Its Peripherals

Networks are designed primarily for two reasons—to allow multiple users to share resources and peripherals, and to allow those users to communicate with one another.

On most networks, at least the ones where someone is concerned about security, before you can start using any network resources or peripherals, you need to log in. When you log in to a network, you usually enter a network ID to identify yourself to the network and then enter a password. The password is part of the security system. Passwords are meant to be kept secret so that any files or other resources you use on the network can be kept confidential.

Your network administrator usually assigns your login ID. IDs can be any combination of characters, and often are in the form of GALENG or GGRIMES. Passwords on the other hand are the creation and responsibility of each user. Different network operating systems have different minimum requirements for user passwords. Some NOSs are created with minimum password requirements, and the LAN administrator sets some password requirements.

Contact your network administrator if you forget your login ID, or need a new one.

Basic Survival

User Passwords

On most networks, passwords are required to be a minimum of five characters. Most security experts argue that you need to make your password a minimum of six characters. You should adhere to the following suggestions when creating a password, to prevent someone from guessing or "hacking" your password:

- Don't use common names such as nicknames, children's names, or pets' names as your password.

- Use a combination of letters and numbers in your password, such as `clarinet23` or `sunshine47`.

- Try to use characters other than letters or numbers in your password, such as `dollar$bird` or `july#56`.

- Don't use birth dates or Social Security numbers as passwords.

- Try to combine unrelated words as passwords, such as `bird%square` or `blue@bovine`.

- Don't reuse old passwords.

- Change your password at least every 30 days.

Accessing Network Drives and Printers

When you access a network drive, the network operating system working with your network client software makes the network drive appear the same as a local drive. As far as you're concerned, the network drive is just another drive letter on your PC. But depending on the access rights your LAN administrator has granted you on that network drive, you may be limited to merely opening and reading existing files on that drive instead of being able to create, delete, and change files.

Accessing a network printer is also very similar to accessing a printer directly connected to your PC. The main difference is that when you send your print job to a network printer, that printer can be located anywhere on the network and does not have to be connected to your PC.

Print jobs in the queue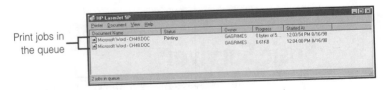

Because there are often numerous network users sending print jobs to the same printer, the printer is often busy when one or more users has sent a print job. The print queue is a holding area for print jobs waiting to be printed. The queue is a FIFO (first in first out) queue. This means that the first print job placed into the queue is the first print job sent to the printer to be printed.

Beyond Survival

Mapping Additional Network Drives

Your network administrator usually sets a certain number of network drives and network printers that you access when you log in to your network. These connections are usually made automatically when you log in by means of a login script.

You can, however, add additional drives to your list of network drives if you have the proper access rights to the drive or directory you want to map to. In many cases, some network users map a drive to a directory that is several levels below where they are mapped to in the login script.

For example, suppose you are mapped to a shared network drive S: and you regularly store files to a directory S:\ACCOUNTING\MONTHLY\BILLING. It would be easier if you could map an additional network drive directly to ..\BILLING so you would not have to spend time navigating down to that directory every time you wanted to save or retrieve a file.

Following is how to map that additional network drive:

1. From the Start menu, select Programs, Windows Explorer to start the Windows Explorer program.

2. Open the Tools menu and select Map Network Drive.

3. In the Drives drop-down list box, select a drive letter that is currently unused (that is, a drive letter that is not used as a local drive, or that is not already mapped to another network drive).

4. In the Path text box, enter the full path to the directory you want to map our new network drive to, in the format \\file server\directory path. For example, if you are mapping to the directory ..\FILES\ACCTG\ MONTHLY\BILLING on file server SARATOGA, you would enter \\SARATOGA\FILES\ACCTG\ MONTHLY\BILLING in the Path text box. Be sure to enter the two preceding backslashes (\\) before the name of the file server.

5. If you want this drive to be mapped automatically every time you log in, be sure to select the Reconnect at logon check box.

6. Click OK, and in a few seconds you should see your newly mapped network drive appear in Windows Explorer.

Cheat Sheet

Common Network Problems

Learn to differentiate between client PC-based network problems and server or systemwide network problems. Some clues you can look for include the following:

- If your PC is the only PC in the immediate area experiencing the problem, then you probably are having a problem with your client PC setup.
- Check to make sure all cables are plugged in to your network interface card and that no files have been deleted.
- If other users are experiencing problems such as not being able to log in to the network, then chances are the problem is not with your client PC but with the servers or network infrastructure.

56

Potential Network Problems

Working on a PC network is not without its share of problems. With all of the hardware and software that must work in tandem, it's not very difficult, as they say, to "...throw a monkey wrench into the works."

Basic Survival

It may come as a surprise to many that the greatest source of problems is human error—what some call a "one-D-ten-T" (hint: Remove the spelling and write the numbers) error. And probably at the top of the list are password-related problems.

On some networking systems, passwords are case sensitive, and on others they are not. To avoid this type of problem, you should always make sure your Caps Lock key is off. Whenever you change your password, make sure you enter only lowercase letters unless you specifically intend to enter uppercase letters.

Another frequent cause of networking problems centers on missing or deleted files that make up your network client software. Occasionally, users see a directory on their hard disk they don't remember creating and decide to delete the files to free some disk space. Unfortunately, those files are needed the next time the user attempts to log in to their LAN. It's always a good idea to ask first before deleting files on your hard disk that you didn't create and aren't sure what their purpose is.

Another source of networking problems you may encounter are hardware related. Network interface cards do occasionally fail, but some apparent failures are user created in origin. A common "apparent" failure is caused by a loose or accidentally removed cable. Unless you are operating on a wireless network, you have a cable connected to the back of your PC that is plugged in to your network interface card. A loose cable or a cable that has been accidentally removed appears as a network failure. If you can't log in to your network, make sure the cable is still plugged in to your network card. Also, check to see whether the other end of the cable is plugged into your network jack.

Network-related problems don't end simply because you successfully connect and log in to your network. In the last chapter, you learned how to map additional network drives. Don't get carried away with mapping additional network drives. Although there is naturally a limit of 26 minus the number of local drives installed on your PC, some networks impose a smaller maximum number of mapped network drives. You should also be aware that every network drive you maintain uses some of your PC's available memory and system resources and slows your PC's performance.

The same warning applies to connecting to network printers. Don't connect to every printer you see. Each connection to a network printer also requires a small amount of memory.

Beyond Survival

More Complex Network Problems

Most other network-related problems are generally beyond your ability to control or repair, but you should still be aware of some of the types of problems that can appear.

Most of the other network problems you may be affected by originate with your file servers. File servers can experience many of the same types of problems as standard PCs. Chief among these problems is that file servers do occasionally crash.

File servers can crash for a variety of reasons:

- A bug in a program that the file server is running causes the server to crash.

- Programs use memory in such a way that the server runs out of available memory to run additional programs or perform server operations, and eventually the file server crashes.

- A hardware component such as a disk drive, controller card, or network interface card fails and crashes the server.

There's practically nothing you can do if the server crashes, because that realm of network operations is out of the control of the users. Just remember—if your PC is the only one having problems, the problem is probably localized to your PC. But, if every user in your immediate area is experiencing the same problem, chances are the problem does not reside with your PC but is a more extensive network-related problem.

Servers aren't the only infrastructure components that can fail and cause network problems. Hubs, routers, bridges, and cabling can also fail and prevent large numbers of users from logging in or accessing network resources.

Index

compact, 19, 210
copying files, 124,
127-128
defragmenting, 232-235
ejecting, 18
floppy
as source of viruses, 227
copying files, 124,
127-128
ejecting, 18
formatting, 16, 20
inserting, 18
scanning for viruses, 229
viewing, 111
formatting, 16, 20
inserting, 18-19
restoring, 248-249, 251
startup, creating, 238-241
storage, networks, 310
viewing, 111, 144, 147
display, changing, 162,
166-168
displaying
Channel Bar, 180-182
desktop, 36
documents, 98
drives, 16, 19-20
files and folders, 106-110
memory, amount of, 14
print queue, 217
processor type, 14
properties, 144-147
Start menu, 40
windows, 51, 53
documents
closing, 94, 96
creating, 94, 96
displaying, 98
opening, 60, 62, 94-95
previewing, 100, 102
printing, 100-101
renaming, 88, 90
saving, 88-91
setting up pages, 100, 102
switching among, 97
Documents command, 41
DOS, 71, 224

DOS command, 74
dot-matrix printers, 6, 11
double-clicking, 6, 10
dragging, 6, 10, 124-125
drawing programs
function of, 22, 27
Paint, 72
drives
CD-ROM, 16, 18-19
defined, 17
disk, 6-7, 16-18
DVD-ROM, 16, 19
ejecting floppy
disks from, 18
finding, 16, 19-20
floppy, 16-17
inserting disks into, 18-19
networks, 314-316
viewing, 16
Zip, 17
drop-down list boxes, 44, 48
DVD-ROM drives, 16, 19

E

editing color schemes and
patterns, desktop, 170-172
educational software, 22, 27
ejecting floppy disks, 18
electrical outlets, 29
ellipses, 46
email
as source of viruses, 227
purpose of, 266
responding to, 291
servers, 307
emptying Recycle Bin,
130, 132
erasing
files, 130-131, 221
folders, 114, 116
programs, Start menu,
154, 157
shortcuts, 150, 153
text, 80-81
ergonomical keyboards, 9

errors, checking for, 220,
222-225
ethernet networks, 300,
303, 305-306
events, adding sounds to,
206-208
Excel, 26
exiting
Active Desktop, 182
documents, 94, 96
email, 291
Help, 54
menus, 46
screen savers, 174, 176
windows, 52
expanding folders, 111
expansion slots, 6-7
Explorer, 71, 106, 110
exploring the Internet,
276-277, 279

F

Favorites command, 41
Favorites list, 276, 279-281
file servers, 300, 302, 304,
306, 311
file types, changing, 91
files
accessing, networks, 302
backing up, 244-246
changing views, 106, 108
copying, 124, 126, 128
creating shortcuts,
150-151
deleting, 130-131
deselecting, 120-121
fragmentation of, 233
inverting selections, 123
missing or deleted, 319
moving, 124-125, 128
pasting, 128
renaming, 134-135
restoring, 248-249, 251
retrieving, Recycle Bin,
130, 132

searching, 138-142
selecting, 120-122
viewing
My Computer, 106-108
properties, 144-146
Windows Explorer, 106, 110
wallpaper, 168-169
financial programs, 26
Find command, 41
finding
drives, 19-20
files and folders, 138-142
Help topics, 54-56
memory, amount of, 14
processor type, 13-14
Web sites, 282
floppy disks
as source of viruses, 227
copying files, 124, 127-128
ejecting, 18
formatting, 16, 20
inserting, 18
scanning for viruses, 229
viewing, 111
floppy drives, 16-17
folders
adding, Start menu, 158-159
changing views, 106, 108
copying, 114, 118
creating, 114-115
deleting, 114, 116
expanding, 111
moving, 116-117, 159
Recycle Bin, 221
renaming, 134-135
searching, 138-142
shortcuts, 150-151
viewing
My Computer, 106-108
properties, 144-146
Windows Explorer, 106, 110
formatting floppy disks, 16, 20

fragmentation of files, 233
Freelance Graphics, 26

G-H

games
function of, 22, 27
Solitaire, 10, 73
gigabytes, 14, 18
graphics, selecting, 76, 78
handling print jobs, 214, 217-218
hard disks
backing up, 244-246
checking for errors, 220, 222-225
clusters, 233
copying files, 124, 127-128
defragmenting, 232-235
restoring, 248-249, 251
viewing, 111
hard drives, 16-18
hardware
Add New Hardware Wizard, 252, 254
defined, 2-3
drives
CD-ROM, 16, 18-19
defined, 17
disk, 6-7, 16-18
DVD-ROM, 16, 19
expansion slots, 6-7
floppy, 16-17
Internet connections, 265
keyboards, 9
memory, 6-7, 13
microprocessors, 6-7, 12-13
modems, 265
monitors, 6, 8-9, 30
motherboards, 6, 8
mouse, 6, 9-10
networks, 300, 302, 304-307, 310-311

placement of, 30
power supply, 7
printers, 6, 11, 214-215, 217
removable media, 247
system box, 7, 11
video cards, 8
Zip, 17
Help, 54-57
Help command, 41
History list, Web sites, 276, 281
hubs, 304, 306-307
human error, 319

I

IBM-compatible computers, 3
icons
changing display, 162, 166-167
desktop, 39
shortcuts, 62, 150-153
Illustrator, 27
images
resolution, 8
selecting, 76, 78
Inbox, 40
index, Help, 54, 57
initializing floppy disks, 16, 20
inkjet printers, 6, 11
inserting disks, 18-19
installing
hardware, Add New Hardware Wizard, 252, 254
Norton AntiVirus, 228
printers, 214-215, 217
programs, 190, 192, 194-195
Windows components, 190, 196
IntelliMouse, 10